DATE DUE

WEST BERLIN: THE LEGAL CONTEXT

A Publication of the
Mershon Center for Education in National Security

West Berlin:

The Legal Context

STANLEY D. METZGER
J. W. BISHOP
HANS W. BAADE
SAUL MENDLOVITZ

Edited by ROLAND J. STANGER

OHIO STATE UNIVERSITY PRESS
1966

Foreword

BERLIN is the epicenter of East-West pressures. Tension can mount and armed conflict break out at other places on the perimeters of the great power blocs, e.g., Greece, Korea, Vietnam; and cold war can intrude, if either side chooses that it should, even in such remote areas as the Congo. For Berlin, geography alone is enough to insure continuous tension and the constant threat of armed conflict: armed conflict not between surrogates, but directly between the United States and Russia, and all that that implies. Geography also gives the initiative primarily to the East and limits the West largely to a choice between less than satisfactory responses to Communist moves.

Whether the victorious allies, when they created the Berlin enclave deep in the Russian sector and provided for its joint occupation, were aware how controversy-prone the situation would be, is debatable. It seems doubtful that any of the statesmen involved foresaw the intensity of the cold war or the urgent necessity to minimize the risks of a Russo-American confrontation, given the soul-sickening consequences of thermonuclear war. It may be, then, that the occupation arrangements were motivated primarily by the need to provide for the government of defeated Germany and, by *de facto* partition pending a more permanent solution, to insure that a resurgent Germany did not again plunge Europe and the world into war. A further factor was, however, certainly at work in some degree. Neither Russia nor the Western Allies could countenance the possibility that the full power of a united Germany should be pre-empted by the other side. This factor has, in the intervening years, clearly become dominant. It may be, as Professor Metzger vigorously contends, that "the division of Germany and of Berlin represents now, as it has done since 1945, a more satisfactory settlement than any other which the Western and Eastern wartime Allies could achieve without war; and that this settlement was sufficiently protective of their interests to be tolerable, or in any event, more tolerable than fighting"; and that efforts to upset it should cease. It seems a fair statement, however, that the history of the years since 1945 has been largely one of the efforts of both East and West to alter the existing balance. The West has had to act with greater caution and subtlety, particularly in Berlin, because its position depends so largely on maintaining, in form, the status quo; Russia can afford to be more venturesome.

No one, least of all the writers of these essays, believes that basically the moves and responses of both East and West have been, or are likely to be, other than politically motivated. The same holds for the restraint shown by both sides, which, in the context, has been great. None believes that the Berlin problem is justiciable in any meaningful sense. But this by no means implies that the course of events has not been influenced and, to some indeterminate degree, shaped by an awareness of, if not a regard for, the relevant rules of international law. The compelling interest of these essays lies in their effort to probe for and to measure this impact of international law, actual and potential, on the Berlin situation.

Historically, the rights of the Western Allies to presence in, and access to, Berlin, and the whole complex of rights of West Berliners, East Berliners, West Germans, East Germans, and the rest to be and move and trade have rested primarily on the rules governing military occupation and the supplementing treaties of the victorious allies. Professor Bishop traces the history of the occupation, sorts out and analyzes the legal issues raised, and concludes that the rights arising from military occupation and the treaties remain relatively intact. Prospectively, however, West Germany and East Germany will demand and play larger and possibly destabilizing roles in Berlin. As Professor Baade's searching analysis makes clear, the legal bases for their claims to be heard depend on a resolution of that complex issue, the status of the Federal Republic of Germany and the German Peoples Republic, and their relationship to the German Reich. Nothing suggests, then, that Berlin will become less risk-prone than it has been since 1945; rather, there are more issues available to those moved to raise them. It is with this in mind that one should read Professor Mendlovitz' ringing challenge to international lawyers to take a new approach to the Berlin problem; an approach that promises a larger role for international law in its resolution; an approach that recognizes its relevance to "the central problem of our time, the prevention of war and the establishment of a peace system for international relations."

These essays were originally presented at the Ohio State University at a regional meeting of the American Society of International Law, cosponsored by the College of Law and the Mershon Committee for Education in National Security. This book is published by the Committee in order that they may reach a wider audience.

ROLAND J. STANGER

Contents

WEST BERLIN: THE LEGAL CONTEXT

The Division of Berlin and of Germany

STANLEY D. METZGER*

A DISCUSSION of the Berlin issue, as of any other, has a purpose, whether that discussion is to be about the political, economic, or legal aspects of the issue, or all three. I take it, therefore, that the purpose of our discussion is to analyze what countries have said and done about Berlin in order to assess the present position and to point the direction, as we see it, in which our policies, political and legal, should be aimed. Berlin having been the capital of Germany, any discussion of its problems necessarily involves the German issue, of which it has been an integral part.

Since the Senate Foreign Relations Committee's publication in December, 1961, of *Documents on Germany, 1944-1961,* consisting of extracts and texts of agreements, notes, memoranda, and related material, runs to a mere 829 pages, and since the memoirs and histories have been cascading upon us for almost two

---

* Professor of Law, Georgetown University Law Center.

decades, it seems clear that rigorous selection and a fairly wide brush must be employed in order to make in brief compass whatever contribution one feels he may have to make to this important question.

Without further ado, then, this paper will argue the following propositions:

1. During and since World War II the victorious Allied Powers arrived at a practical "settlement" of both the Berlin and German issues: the division of Germany and of Berlin on the zonal occupation boundaries between East and West established in 1944-45 and the other territorial dispositions then made.

2. The relative permanence of this settlement of the past eighteen years is attested in part by the failure of efforts to upset it.

3. East and West should desist from further efforts to upset the existing settlement.

With the propositions stated, it is now necessary to set forth reasons for believing them to be valid.

THE 1944-45 "SETTLEMENT" OF THE DIVISION OF GERMANY AND BERLIN ON THE ZONAL OCCUPATION BOUNDARIES

During World War II the principal Allied Powers—the British, the Americans, and the Russians—considered very seriously the formal dismemberment of Germany, even apart from the cession of East Prussia and compensation to Poland for accepting the Curzon line as its eastern boundary.

In the United States, President Roosevelt said, in early October, 1943, that "categorically he favored the partition of Germany into three or more states, completely sovereign."[1] While Secretary Hull, reflecting a position taken at staff levels in the State Department, argued that partition "would have many undesirable results," the President indicated that "the whole transitional period would have to be one of trial and error."[2]

At the Moscow Conference on October 25, 1943, the British view, expressed by Foreign Minister Eden, was that Britain "would not like to see a united Germany remain but would prefer to see her divided into separate states, particularly a separate Prussia." His government would therefore "encourage any separatist tendencies within Germany, but . . . it was divided in its opinion on the desirability of attempting to impose the dismemberment of Germany by forcible means."[3] Molotov, for Russia, merely indicated that the Soviet Union was in favor of all measures that would render Germany harmless in the future. This was marked reticence, since Stalin had told Churchill in December, 1941, that he favored the "detachment of the Rhineland as an independent State or protectorate, and possibly the constitution of an independent State of Bavaria."[4]

Hull, whose personal position was then in opposition to dismemberment (apart from the separation of East Prussia on which all were agreed), stated that his government had been struck by the "widely divergent views among Allied Governments on the subject of dismemberment of Germany." He added, however, (in view of his discussion with the President): "In high quarters in the United States . . . when the study of this problem had begun there had been a general disposition to favor the dismemberment of Germany. But as discussions progressed . . . there was an increasing disposition to keep an open mind on this point and to explore it more fully before determining upon our final attitude—although dismemberment was still in favor."[5]

Although it appears that at the Teheran Conference which met in November, 1943, "the weight of top-level British and American policy was thrown quite explicitly toward one form or another of dismemberment," the open mind referred to by Secretary Hull in Moscow in 1943 was not really closed through the period which culminated in the defeat of Germany and the assumption of supreme authority by the Allied Powers in that country in June, 1945. There were many discussions, however, internal and external.

In the United States serious discussions were further undertaken in early September, 1944, with the early defeat of Germany then thought to be in the offing. The Morgenthau Plan, widely known for its proposal to "pastoralize" Germany, also contained detailed partition provisions: France to get the Saar and adjacent territorities bounded by the Rhine and Moselle rivers; Denmark to get territories north of the Kiel Canal; and the rest of Germany to be divided into three units. These units were an international zone containing the Ruhr, its surrounding industrial areas, and the Kiel Canal (to be run by the United Nations organization to be established) and two autonomous states: one, a south German state comprising Bavaria, Württemberg, Baden, and smaller areas; the other, a north German state comprising a large part of Prussia, Saxony, Thuringia, and smaller states. Hull opposed this part of the plan as well as that portion relating to making Germany agricultural in character, but not nearly so strongly; Secretary of War Stimson, whose opposition to the deindustrialization part of the plan probably had greatest influence upon its later abandonment, actually favored a form of dismemberment.

Hull's position was that, in place of partition, "every effort be made to promote a federal system of government in Germany, and a division of Prussia into a number of medium-sized states."[6] Stimson's was that there be transferred from Germany, "East Prussia, Upper Silesia, Alsace and Lorraine"; he added that "We [the War Department] also are considering the wisdom of a possible partition of Germany into north and south sections, as well as the creation of an internationalized state in the Ruhr."[7]

The Quebec Conference between the U.S. and the U.K. in late 1944, while adopting the "pastoralization" aspect of the Morgenthau Plan (which was later abandoned), did not deal with dismemberment in its dispositive agreement.[8]

Immediately thereafter, in connection with Hull's efforts to upset the apparent decision to pastoralize Germany, he once again, in late October, 1944, addressed himself to the dismemberment question: "No decision should be taken on the possible partition of

Germany, but we should encourage a decentralization of the German governmental structure, and if any tendencies toward spontaneous partition of Germany arose they should not be discouraged." [9]

It should be recalled at this point that in September, 1944, the European Advisory Commission had already delineated the respective occupation zones in Germany and had likewise divided Berlin into three parts to be occupied by the forces of the respective powers. This decision, unlike a decision on dismemberment, was "settled without difficulty." [10]

Hull's position that "no decision should be taken on partition," and the President's agreement with it in October, 1944, must therefore be assessed in terms of this foreknowledge. So also must the President's comment at the time: "In regard to the Soviet Government, it is true that we have no idea as yet what they have in mind, but we have to remember that in their occupied territory they will do more or less as they wish." [11] This judgment was made on September 29, 1944.

That the victorious powers never did depart from their open mind about dismemberment, in the sense of deciding either to require or preclude it, appears from the Yalta Agreement of February, 1945, from the Declaration regarding the Defeat of Germany and the Assumption of Supreme Authority by the Allied Powers in June, 1945, and from the Potsdam Agreement of August, 1945.

However, at least until June, 1945, the tendency was toward formal partition, although without any agreement as to details. Thus, the Yalta Agreement provision on dismemberment provided: "The United Kingdom, the United States of America and the Union of Soviet Socialist Republics shall possess supreme authority in Germany. In the exercise of such authority they will take such steps, including the complete disarmament, demilitarisation and dismemberment of Germany, as they deem requisite for future peace and security." [12]

The June, 1945, Declaration Regarding Germany, however, was somewhat less forthright: "The Governments of the United States of America, the Union of Soviet Socialist Republics and the United Kingdom, and the Provisional Government of the French Republic, will hereafter determine the boundaries of Germany or any part thereof and the status of Germany or any area at present being part of German territory." [13] Perhaps this was a reflection of Roosevelt's death, since he had been "the strongest advocate" [14] of dismemberment, and of the very considerable evolution in Stalin's thinking. For Stalin, perhaps considering that he could always insure his security interests through occupation of the Russian zone and might widen his influence to the whole of Germany, announced to the Russian people on May 8, 1945, that "the Soviet Union does not intend to dismember or destroy Germany." [15]

Potsdam, while providing that during the period of occupation "Germany shall be treated as a single economic unit," also called for "the decentralization of the political structure and the development of local responsibility," and, withal, was silent on the question

9

of whether, or how, Germany should be dismembered.[16] It may, however, have indicated when the partition question would be faced, if ever, by its handling of the German eastern (and Polish western) frontier question. For in agreeing that, pending the final determination of Poland's western frontier, she should have administering authority over former German territories east of the Oder-Neisse line, the Allies also stated that "the final delimitation of the western frontier of Poland should await the peace settlement." [17]

Writing in 1955, former President Truman stated that at the time of Potsdam "my aim was a unified Germany with a centralized government in Berlin." [18] However that may be, there is not a line in Potsdam indicating that the open mind of the Allied Powers on dismemberment, a mind which hitherto had been hospitable to, if not very clear upon, the details of partition, had in any way become fixed upon the idea of unification. It is interesting also to note, as an aside, that on the question of centralized government in Berlin the only disposition in Potsdam was that, although certain essential German administrative departments should be established, "for the time being no central German Government shall be established." [19]

As an astute observer characterized the position at the end of the war, "the situation was as follows. Although Roosevelt's death had eliminated the strongest advocate [of dismemberment], the United States government was still split on the issue of dismemberment. There was an equivalent muddled situation in British

10

policy, although at least some in London . . . already explicitly looked forward to a split of Germany east and west along the line of the Soviet Zone of occupation. . . . The Soviets had gained freedom of action—for propaganda as well as diplomatic purposes—by formally detaching themselves from the tentative Yalta agreement for a form of dismemberment." [20]

Since Potsdam, despite numerous conferences, there has been no peace settlement regarding Germany and no further agreements between East and West regarding either dismemberment or unification. There had not been and there is not today any formal international agreement between East and West determining that Germany shall be a political unit or that it shall be partitioned.

But if there has been no formal agreement, this by no means signifies that a *modus vivendi*, a practical settlement reflecting the realities of power and the avoidance of less desirable alternatives, has also been missing.

The division of Germany and of Berlin decided upon for occupation purposes represented the practical settlement at the close of World War II which the former Allied Powers accepted as less undesirable than other alternative "solutions" might turn out to be. When in 1945 the Allies finally put aside efforts to decide whether and how to partition Germany, they did so in light of the determination of the occupation zones made in September, 1944, and the actual occupation of these zones in 1945: they had a lively appreciation, based upon earlier knowledge and experience, that occupation, like possession, would amount to nine-tenths of the law, making formal partition to a considerable extent an academic exercise.

They were then preoccupied with the desire to avoid witnessing the resurgence of an armed, unified Germany capable once again, through maneuvering in the cockpits of East-West politics, of breaking the peace through seeking European domination at the expense of either East or West, as had twice been sought in this century. German aggression and inhumanity had aroused universal emotions felt, not just by British, Russians, French, and Americans, but by the Dutch, Norwegians, Danes, Belgians, Poles, Czechs, and countless others, including the handful of survivors of, and those who merely had read about, the crematoriums, the Bergen-Belsens, and the Auschwitzes.

The Allied Powers also distrusted each other—Western and Eastern allies—sufficiently to desire that each would not have the untrammeled opportunity to enlist a united Germany on the side of one or the other in any efforts either might make to secure wider dominance than the war had brought them through the efforts of their armed forces in defeating Germany.

What had Berlin to do with this practical division of Germany which was then seen to serve the interests of East and West better than any other upon which they could then find agreement? Berlin was seen then, as it is seen now, as a part of the German problem. When Secretary Herter stated in 1959 that "There can be no lasting solution for Berlin by itself," [21] he was reiterating what had been clear from the outset.

As the capital of Germany, Berlin was a symbol. As the powers had agreed to split Germany for occupation purposes and had put no duration on the occupation, so it appeared sensible for them to split the symbol for the same purposes.

THE PERSISTENCE OF THIS PRACTICAL SETTLEMENT

This practical settlement—the division of Germany— has not been free from efforts from various quarters to upset it during these past eighteen years. Twice the Russians sought to expel the West from Berlin: once in the 1948 Berlin blockade and once in a continuing effort beginning in 1958 which has become less strenuous since the erection of the wall bounding the Russian occupation area.

It is never easy to assess the weight of motives for international actions which can involve more than one. It is likely but not certain that the motive in 1948 represented another in the Russian moves of that day to expel the United States from Europe in order to hasten the day when Russian influence could spread further westward. It is likely but not certain that the motive since 1958 has been another in a series of moves to cement Soviet influence in the area where it secured influence in consequence of the services of its arms during World War II, in view of the relative attractions of Western economic and social development as compared with that of the Eastern areas and countries under Soviet influence.

In any event, whatever the dominant motivation, the Russians were unwilling in the end to make war to have their way, which it appeared they would need to do because the West was unwilling to let them have their way otherwise. And they desisted. In this connection it is difficult to see anything of substance in the war of words about the West's right of access to its occupation areas in Berlin because of some alleged failure to specify in writing such rights. In 1958 the Department of State stated that "The right of each power to be in occupation of Berlin is of the same standing as the right of each power to be in occupation of its zone. Further, the rights of the three Western Powers to free access to Berlin as an essential corollary of their right of occupation there is of the same stature as the right of occupation itself." [22] I think this was and is clearly right.

But the Russian efforts to upset the practical settlement of the division of Germany and of Berlin were not the only essays in this endeavor. The Western powers, at first in 1946 (the early days of occupation), and then again in 1953, in 1955, and in 1959, pressed for the unification of Germany in negotiations with Russia and in public statements. The positions of West and East in these protracted bouts of negotiations and propaganda exercises soon achieved the status of formulas: the West called for free all-German elections and then a peace treaty with an elected German government; the East called for a negotiated German government comprising representation from West and East Germany, followed by a peace treaty. It didn't take very long for each to know perfectly that its position was unacceptable to the other, but this didn't seem to prevent one from continuing to urge that position upon the other until the world became utterly bored. The 1959 "negotiations," the latest in what seemed to be a never-ending series, at least resulted in the participants themselves becoming so bored that we have been spared these exercises since then. From time to time ideas of "neutralizing" and demilitarizing a unified Germany were put forward, but these too foundered because neither East nor West really believed the Germans could be relied upon to stay neutral or demilitarized, or that they could rely upon each other in the event she did not. It would be difficult to fault either West or East on this score.

Why did the West appear to press for unification, which would of course have upset the division of Germany and Berlin? Again, the real motivations are never wholly clear, and they may well have varied depending upon which part of the West one had in mind. It is not easy to believe, for example, that the Dutch and the Belgians were eager to see Germany reunified and at the same time were anxious to see Britain in the Common Market, partly to offset the strong influence of a non-unified West Germany. It is also not difficult to wonder about the motivations of the French and the British, both of whom appear to have had reason to view with askance a united Germany of eighty million strong in the heart of Europe. After all, "the permanent dilemma of French policy," as Anthony Eden put it, was "whether Russia or Germany was more to be feared." [23] The French, in fact, had argued most strenuously in 1946 for the detachment of the Ruhr from the rest of Germany but had lost. And Britain has for centuries been concerned with the domination of Europe by one power; the pos-

15

sibility of a united Germany being that power has in this century been more foreboding than others, at least until the Russian threat, and perhaps also since the Russian threat has appeared to the British to have subsided.

All this might signify that the European support for the American-inspired drive for a unified Germany was forthcoming only because the Europeans knew that the Russians would reject the idea and that there was no intention of fighting a war for unification, which they also knew the Russians knew. At the same time, their public willingness to see Germany unified enabled them to say to the Germans, for whatever profit there might be in it, that it was plain to see that only the Russians were stopping unification. I have always doubted whether this gambit, if it was in fact employed in this instance, has been as successful as its constant use would seem to indicate. Perhaps its real utility is that the assumed beneficiary himself wants an excuse for inaction, not that he is taken in.

As for the United States, for a time, particularly in 1953, one might have thought that there was some important opinion which viewed German unification as a first step toward "liberation" of Eastern Europe. But there was little indication that President Eisenhower had firm views in that direction, and no action based upon such a conception in fact took place. Apart from that, American motivation appeared to be based upon the belief that a unified Germany could help to stem what appeared in the late 1940's to be a strong Russian tide westward. The Europeans, for that matter, might well have shared this view, at least until Stalin's death in 1953, and possibly even until the 1955 summit meeting.

In any event, and whatever the motivations, the events of the past eighteen years have made it clear that, regarding Germany and Berlin, neither East nor West was prepared to fight for objectives beyond what each had secured, and each was believed by the other to be prepared to fight to keep what it held. It therefore appears that the division of Germany and of Berlin represents now, as it has done since 1945, a more satisfactory settlement than any other which the Western and Eastern wartime Allies could achieve without war and that this settlement has been and remains sufficiently protective of their interests to be tolerable, or in any event, more tolerable than fighting.

Further Eastern and Western Efforts to Upset the Settlement

In 1959, at the last of the "negotiations" on Germany and Berlin, former Secretary Herter said: "The division of Germany creates an unnatural situation. Millions of Germans are separated from relatives, friends . . . and fellow countrymen by this artificial separation." [24] Chairman Khrushchev is reported to have said that Berlin was a bone in his throat, and President Eisenhower characterized it as "abnormal." All statements signify a certain unhappiness with the existing division of Germany and of Berlin.

17

There are many situations in history, some quite recent, which might be considered by some to be "unnatural" but to which countries tend to become accustomed and in time consider quite appropriate. North and South Korea, North and South Vietnam, separated East and West Pakistan, to name only a few, no doubt are as unnatural as the division of Germany. At one time the United States thought that it was quite natural for it to expand to latitude 54° 40′, or fight. When the British and Canadians indicated that, natural or not, they chose not to oblige, and the United States decided not to fight very much, the United States managed to get along quite nicely in its present borders. We've heard no more of the artificiality of our borders for some time now.

It is very difficult to deal meaningfully with this "naturalness" of borders question. Hitler thought it natural for Germany to have the Sudetenland, plus Austria, plus Danzig, because there were Germans there who were relatives, friends, or fellow Germans, and that it was also natural to have the Ukraine because there were only Russians there and they could be decimated in order to make room for Germans. Perhaps a future German government, East or West, will consider it natural to resecure East Prussia or Alsace-Lorraine.

If what Mr. Herter meant to say was that there has been a tendency on the part of ethnically similar people to get together, history can be called as witness. History can also attest, however, many examples of ethnically similar people resisting amalgamation, and still more of ethnically dissimilar people seeking domination over one another.

But let us suppose the division of Germany is in some sense unnatural and the division of Berlin is in some sense abnormal, just as the division of North and South Korea may in some sense be considered artificial.

Does this mean that it makes sense to continue to try to upset this settlement? Is American or European security in danger because of a divided Germany? Is Russian security in danger because of a divided Berlin? Is West Germany starving, or is she in such good economic shape that she exports capital to the United States as well as other areas? Is East Germany so injured that she has been unable to make an economic life, or is she the fourth-largest industrial power in Europe?

On the other hand, could the United States and Europe reasonably consider that the balance of power was being upset by the first step of being driven from Berlin? Could the Russians reasonably consider that a unification of Germany under existing circumstances might be the first step toward undermining what she considers to be her legitimate security interests?

With nations as with people, "naturalness" is often curbed when broader interests, such as community welfare or world peace, are at stake. It is probably natural, in some sense of the term, to drive ninety miles an hour in a three-hundred-horsepower automobile, but some organized societies tend to view such behavior with disfavor. This is especially true when we speak of Germany, whose behavior, however you wish to describe it in terms of naturalness, for some time has been dangerous and unsightly. If there is anything that is natural in our subject, I should suppose it to be the natural reaction of millions of people and many nations to wish to curb the recent propensity of Germany to despoil, to destroy, and to denigrate the human spirit, and to do this by seeking to keep it from becoming again so strong as, either by itself or in some combination, again to break the peace.

The effort may of course fail. But is it not in the interest of the former Allies at the least to cease and desist from upsetting the division of Germany and of Berlin? In this connection it is encouraging that the United States has not resumed pressure for unification and that Russia has greatly softened its demands that the Western powers leave Berlin, hopefully in anticipation of dropping them altogether. In fact, events of the 1963–65 period have generally been helpful on this score.

We are a good deal better off today on the German issue than we were at a comparable period after World War I. Eighteen years after World War I was 1936, the year Hitler marched into the Rhineland, the year before he marched into Vienna, two years before he marched to Prague, and three years before he descended upon Warsaw. The practical settlement of the German and Berlin issue by division on the lines of the occupation zones and the maintenance of this settlement by the determination of West and East to resist each other's pressures to upset it have contributed immeasurably during these past eighteen years to the great improvement in which we find ourselves today on the German problem as compared with that which existed after a comparable period following World War I.

If there could be a surcease altogether from efforts to upset the present settlement of the German and Berlin issue and perhaps, although this may be too much to hope, a mutual determination to uphold it, we should all be still better off.

1. 2 HULL, MEMOIRS OF CORDELL HULL 1265 (1948) [hereinafter referred to as HULL MEMOIRS]. This represented a hardening of his attitude expressed to Foreign Minister Anthony Eden of Great Britain in March, 1943, which was that "under any circumstance, Germany must be divided into several states," but there should not be dictated an "arbitrary" division of Germany that did not spring from German public opinion. The difference was that by October the President believed that the separate states should be "completely sovereign." See SHERWOOD, ROOSEVELT AND HOPKINS 711 (1948), quoted in ROSTOW, THE UNITED STATES IN THE WORLD ARENA 96 (1960).

2. 2 HULL MEMOIRS 1265.

3. *Ibid.* at 1287.

4. 3 CHURCHILL, THE SECOND WORLD WAR 558 (1950).

5. 2 HULL MEMOIRS 1287.

6. 2 HULL MEMOIRS 1607.

7. STIMSON AND BUNDY, ON ACTIVE SERVICE IN PEACE AND WAR 572 (1948).

8. *Ibid.* at 576–77.

9. 2 HULL MEMOIRS 1619.

10. ROSTOW, *op. cit. supra* note 1, at 98.

11. 2 HULL MEMOIRS 1620-21.

12. STAFF OF SENATE COMM. ON FOREIGN RELATIONS, 87TH CONG., 1ST SESS., DOCUMENTS ON GERMANY 1944–1961, 8 (Comm. Print 1961), [hereinafter cited as DOCUMENTS].

13. DOCUMENTS 13.

14. ROSTOW, *op. cit. supra* note 1, at 97.

15. *Ibid.*

16. DOCUMENTS 32–33.

17. DOCUMENTS 37–38.

18. TRUMAN MEMOIRS 306 (1955).

19. DOCUMENTS 32.

20. ROSTOW, *op. cit. supra* note 1, at 97.

21. Foreign Ministers' Meeting, May–August, 1959, DEP'T. STATE PUB. No. 6882 at 9.

22. DOCUMENTS 373.

23. EDEN, FULL CIRCLE 52 (1960).

24. Foreign Ministers' Meeting, May–August, 1959, DEP'T. STATE PUB. No. 6882 at 10.

The Origin and Nature of the Rights of the Western Allies in Berlin*

J. W. Bishop†

A NECESSARY PRELIMINARY to a discussion of the legal status of Berlin is a consideration of the question whether these points of law really matter and, if they do, why. The Soviet government did not attempt to strangle the city in 1948 because a study of treatises on international law had convinced it that the Western Allies had no legal right to remain in the city, and it did not give up that attempt because the cogent arguments of Western lawyers had persuaded it otherwise. The Russians turned off the blockade because it was not working and because the Allied counterblockade was putting a severe strain on the feeble economy of East Germany. (Of course, it may well be argued that the abandonment of the blockade itself proved something about the rights of the parties in the city, just as the event at Appomatox elucidated once and for all

* This article was based upon a lecture delivered in April, 1963.
† Professor of Law, Yale University Law School.

some basic questions of Constitutional law which had theretofore been regarded as at least doubtful.) At no time since 1958, when the U.S.S.R., announcing that it could no longer tolerate the Western occupation of Berlin, inaugurated the flexible campaign of pressure, threats, sweet reasonableness, and blackmail which has continued intermittently to the present day, did Mr. Khrushchev evince any disposition to take the case to the International Court of Justice. For that matter, neither did Mr. Kennedy, or even Mr. Macmillan, and centainly not General de Gaulle or Dr. Adenauer. And yet all of the governments concerned have clogged the air waves and stuffed diplomatic pouches with thousands of words intended to demonstrate that international law solidly supports, on the one hand, the exclusion of the Western forces from Berlin and, on the other, their continued presence there. My own file, which is very far from complete, contains several hundred pages of the tedious, repetitious, and somewhat flatulent notes, aide-memoires, memoranda, etc., etc.— all of them heavily larded with the legal argumentation in which the disputants have put their cases to each other and the rest of the world. I may note in passing that they make very hard and indigestible reading indeed. I am not privy to the contents of the apparently interminable talks between the Soviet and American governments which started in 1961 and which, after a recess for the Cuban crisis, have now been resumed; I think it safe to guess that much of what has been said has a strong legal flavor.

24

Thus, I am brought up short at the outset of this examination of the law of the case by the question of *why* parties who will not go to court have put so many lawyers to work. The question, of course, is one which bedevils any consideration of international law in the context of an actual and important dispute between nations, and of course I can give no pat answer. The best I can do is to suggest that the motives of Messrs. Kennedy, Khrushchev, *et al.* were not essentially different from those which led the saintly statesmen of the Papacy, in the darkest of the dark ages, to forge the Donation of Constantine as a legal basis for their claims to temporal sovereignty. (I do not suggest, of course, that any of the present disputants have actually resorted to such doctoring of the record.) Men who are even moderately civilized prefer, by long habit and training, to have the law on their side, even if there are no policemen to enforce that law. Moreover, neither the NATO powers nor the Communists have any desire to seem lawless in the eyes of the neutral nations or their own people. Indeed, I think there is more to it than a mere desire to keep up appearances. One of the many qualities which made Adolf Hitler unique among modern rulers was his quite genuine and open contempt for law, domestic or international. He really seems never to have bothered to convince himself that what he wanted to do had any legal justification. But the heads of state chiefly concerned in the present dispute appear to be essentially sane and normal men, and I suspect that each of them, including the Soviet leaders, prefers to believe, and probably does believe, that his political goals and his methods of achieving them are legal and even equitable. In general, the Communists are probably a good deal less devoted to the concept of the rule of law than are democratic statesmen, but in a batch, selected more or less at random, of four speeches made by Mr. Khrushchev at the height of the Berlin crisis of the summer of 1961, I find no less than fourteen appeals to international law, which in each case turned out to support the Soviet position. It goes without saying that these contentions have not passed unchallenged by the West. Indeed, about the only propositions on which the two sides concur is that West Berlin is now under military occupation by the armed forces of France, the United Kingdom, and the United States and that its situation is peculiar.

Let us try then, as dispassionately and objectively as possible, to assess the legal situation. That, of course, requires a statement of the facts. Those facts are pretty well known and, generally speaking, are not in dispute. For present purposes they can be summarized with comparative brevity. The same thing is true of the contents of the various documents which are relevant to the question of the right of the Western powers to be in Berlin;[1] there has been no opportunity, and perhaps no occasion, for fakery.

By late fall of 1943 the defeat of Germany seemed sufficiently certain to call for advance planning of the occupation. The United States, the United Kingdom, and the Soviet Union at the Moscow Foreign Ministers

Conference, held in October of that year, set up the European Advisory Commission (composed of representatives of the three prospective victors), whose job was to recommend terms of surrender and methods of enforcing Allied policy in Germany. Its terms of reference optimistically assumed a joint, tripartite occupation and a joint, tripartite policy. By the fall of 1944 it was apparent to almost everyone except Adolf Hitler and the more bemused of his disciples that the disintegration of the thousand-year Reich was imminent. On September 12, 1944, the three powers signed a protocol, prepared by the European Advisory Commission, providing for the division of Germany into three zones of occupation, one per ally, "and a special Berlin area, which will be under joint occupation by the three powers." In November of the same year this was supplemented by an agreement among the three powers on control machinery for Germany, also prepared by the Advisory Commission. That agreement created the Allied Control Council, composed of the military governors of the three zones of occupation, and an "Inter-Allied Governing Authority"—the so-called *Komendatura* [2]—consisting of the military commandants in each sector of the city, to rule Berlin, subject to the general direction of the Control Council. Each Berlin commandant governed his nation's sector, subject, of course, to the direction of his nation's commander-in-chief in Germany; "questions of principle and problems common to all zones" (i.e., sectors of the city) were to be decided by the Komendatura. As might have been expected, both the Control Council and the Komendatura, like the Security Council of the United Nations, could act only by unanimous vote. It is somewhat remarkable that the application of the veto principle to the workings of the Komendatura was not made explicit until July 7, 1945, although it was no doubt implicit in the subjection of that body to the direction of the Control Council. In July, 1945, these agreements were amended to include France as a fourth occupant of both Berlin and Germany. Its zone and sector were carved out of those allotted to the other two Western powers, and the addition of French members to the Control Council and the Komendatura did not, of course, affect the fundamental balance of power between the Western allies and the Soviet Union—or at least has not so far done so.

When the Nazi government finally evaporated and the four powers, on June 5, 1945, assumed "supreme authority with respect to Germany," the Red Army was in exclusive possession of Berlin. Why that was so has been the subject of a good deal of non-legal discussion, most of it partisan and polemical. General Eisenhower, who ought to know, says that he had decided, for military reasons, that the city "was not the logical or the most desirable objective for the forces of the Western Allies." [3] On the other hand, United States forces occupied most of Saxony and Thuringia to the Elbe River, some 200 miles inside the Russian zone. On June 14 President Truman offered Stalin a trade whereby the American forces would be pulled back to their own zone "in accordance with arrangements between the respective commanders, including in these arrangements simultaneous movement of the national garrisons into Greater Berlin and provision of free access for United forces by air, road and rail to Berlin from Frankfurt and Bremen." Stalin accepted, agreeing to take "all necessary measures" in accordance with the plan. Similar agreements were concluded between Stalin and Churchill—against the better judgment of the latter prescient statesman, for he had viewed the location of the United States forces as conferring a heaven-sent opportunity for "the settlement of many great things which would be the true foundation of world peace," i.e., an opportunity to bargain, realistically and from a position of strength, with the Russians on some of the questions of the future of Germany which the various protocols and declarations had passed over in silence or wrapped in woolly ambiguities.[4] In the immediate succeeding weeks the four zone commandants filled in the details of these basic agreements by arranging for the use by Western forces of the Helmstedt-Berlin railroad and Autobahn, these being the most direct routes across the Soviet zone to Berlin. Access was to be subject only to "normal traffic regulations," which, as General Clay recalled Marshall Zhukov's oral gloss, would include such matters as road signs and document checking, "but no inspection of cargo—the U.S.S.R. is not interested in what is being hauled, how much or how many trucks are moving."[5] By November, 1945, quadripartite agreements had created three air corridors across the Russian zone to Berlin with unrestricted flight, subject only to agreed safety regulations. There were in addition less impor-

29

tant agreements dealing with canal traffic, mail, telephone and telegraph, and so forth.

These fundamental agreements obviously left open many topics for future discussion and agreement. Nevertheless, particularly with respect to Western access to Berlin, they were reasonably explicit and unambiguous. They were at least adequate to the situation with which they were intended to deal and for the assumptions upon which they were predicated. Those assumptions appear clearly in other contemporary agreements. The United States, at least, and probably the British, supposed that the situation was essentially what it had been after World War I and after most previous wars: a military occupation of comparatively short duration—perhaps five years—followed by the establishment of a new central German government with its capital in Berlin and the termination of the occupation by a peace treaty with that new German government. Thus, the agreement of November 14, 1944, which created the Control Council and the Komendatura specified that they were to "operate during the initial period of the occupation of Germany immediately following surrender," and "the question of the Allied organs required for carrying out the functions of control and administration in Germany at a later period" was left to subsequent agreement. The closest thing to such a subsequent agreement is the Potsdam Protocol of August 2, 1945, which has not proved to be very close. Although the heads of state grandly announced in that Protocol agreement "on the political and economic principles of a coordinated Allied policy toward defeated Germany during the period of Allied control," they did nothing further to define how that control was to work. They dealt with the problem of the creation of a new German government by postponing it: "For the time being no central German government shall be established"—although they agreed to set up "essential central German administrative departments" to handle economic matters (finance, transport, trade, etc.) under the direction of the Control Council, which, it will be recalled, could only act unanimously. The problems of ending the occupation and signing a peace treaty were postponed even further; the newly created Council of Foreign Ministers (which replaced the European Advisory Commission) was instructed to prepare "a peace settlement for Germany to be accepted by the government of Germany when a government adequate for the purpose is established." In short, the parties set up temporary arrangements for the occupation of the defeated enemy and agreed to agree later on the long-range solution.

I think it not beyond the bounds of possibility that the Russians themselves shared the optimistic illusion that some such solution might actually be reached. As is well known, one who properly applies the science of Marxism-Leninism cannot err in political diagnosis; but as is also well known (since 1953), the late J. V. Stalin occasionally displayed a defective understanding of Marxism-Leninism. Communists, like other men, often come to believe their own slogans, and it may be that the Russians really did suppose that the German Communist Party could clamber into control of

31

the central government with no more than an initial leg-up from the Red Army. If that had happened—and it is very easy to forget how likely it seemed, before the Marshall Plan, that the Communists really might win elections all over Western Europe—it might have been very difficult for the United States and Great Britain to refuse to sign a peace treaty with the new and honestly elected German government. The point is that the present legal situation of Berlin was not planned by lawyers; it was not planned by Americans, Englishmen, or Frenchmen; and it was probably not planned by Russians. It just happened—as is the case with many other tangled legal problems. Moreover, it is unprecedented. The original interest and policy of the United States, to which it still clings in all its formal pronouncements, was to arrange for the occupation and reconstruction of Germany, pending the creation of a new central government and a peace treaty. Two-thirds of Germany has now been reconstructed to our satisfaction, and the other third to Soviet satisfaction. The problems implicit in mixing this oil and water to produce an homogenous, reunified whole need not be stated in this paper. The United States real policy now, as far as it has one, is to keep the people of West Berlin out of the clutches of the German Democratic Republic.

The original assumptions of quadripartite control of Germany and the creation of a central German government broke down early, because of the total inability of the four victorious powers to agree on anything at all. That history is well known and need not be recapitulated here. Developments in the Berlin microcosm naturally paralleled those in Germany as a whole—and, incidentally, furnish some support to the hypothesis that the Soviet Union, like the West, entered into the arrangements of 1944 and 1945 on the basis of a major political miscalculation. The Russians had utilized their brief period of exclusive occupation to instal in Berlin a German administration dominated by the Socialist Unity (Communist) Party. In October, 1946, the Russians made the never-to-be-repeated mistake of permitting honest elections in Greater Berlin; the Socialist Unity Party took a fearful drubbing, and the German administration of the city became anti-Communist. The Soviet authorities were reduced to the chronic use of the veto in the Komendatura, which (like the Allied Control Council) practically ceased to function. The Soviet delegation formally walked out of the Komendatura on July 1, 1948, the immediate cause being the introduction into West Berlin of the currency reform already effected in the Western zones. These developments were accompanied by the blockade (and counterblockade) of 1948 and the Berlin airlift. In November of the same year the Russians set up a Magistrat (city government) in their sector, purportedly the lawful government of the whole city. The original Magistrat moved to West Berlin, where it has functioned ever since. Thus, there were and are two separate and hostile city governments, each claiming to be the lawful government of Greater Berlin and each, of course, exercising actual authority only in its own bailiwick.

The Western Allies, of course, promptly and repeatedly denounced the blockade as a violation of their rights stemming from the defeat and surrender of Germany—rights of access to Berlin which, they argued, were not only implicit in their status as military occupants of the city but confirmed both by the agreements already described and by usage. The Russians did not —and apparently do not to this day—deny the existence of these agreements nor even seriously contest the construction given them by the West. *Their* legal answer was—and is—that the four-power agreements on Berlin were no more than an "inseparable component part" of the broader agreements on Germany as a whole and that the frustration of these agreements by the Western powers—particularly their transformation of their zones into a separate economic and political unit and their failure to carry out the disarmament of Germany—destroyed the whole system of four-power agreements on Germany and "thereby undermined as well the legal basis which assured their right to participation in the administration of Berlin."

This dispute, it goes without saying, was not resolved by the two quadripartite agreements—the last agreements which seem relevant—made in connection with the ending of the blockade. That of May 4, 1949, simply provided for the simultaneous removal of "all the restrictions imposed since March 1, 1948, by the Government of the Union of Soviet Socialist Republics on communications, transportation, and trade between Berlin and the Western zones of Germany and between the Eastern zone and the Western zones" and the corresponding restrictions placed by the West on such traffic. On June 20, 1949, the four powers agreed that the May agreement should be "maintained." They announced their intention "to continue their efforts to achieve the restoration of the economic and political unity of Germany" and to that end to consult together "to mitigate the effects of the present administrative division of Germany and Berlin," particularly by (a) "Expansion of trade and development of the financial and economic relations between the Western zones and Berlin and between Berlin and the zones"; (b) "Facilitation of the movement of persons and goods and the exchange of information between the Western zones and the Eastern zone and between Berlin and the zones"; and (c) "Consideration of questions of common interest relating to the administration of the four sectors with a view to normalizing as far as possible the life of the city." They agreed further that, in order to promote these laudable purposes "and in order to improve and supplement this and other arrangements and agreements as regard the movement of persons and goods and communications between the Eastern zone and the Western zones and between the zones and Berlin and also in regard to transit, the occupation authorities, each in his own zone, will have an obligation to take the measures necessary to insure the normal functioning and utilization of rail, water and road transport" for the movement of persons and goods between East and West zones and between the zones and Berlin. Nothing was said about air traffic (presumably because it had not been affected by the blockade), and no time limit was set on the "maintenance" of the agreement to lift the blockade.

Despite these virtuous intentions, or at any rate virtuous protestations, the polarization of Germany proceeded apace. In September, 1949, the Federal Republic of Germany was established in the Western zones and accorded a high degree of autonomy, though the occupation was not ended.[6] A week or so later the German Democratic Republic appeared in the East zone and got about the same degree of autonomy as other Communist states in Eastern Europe.[7] But both sides were chary of drastic tampering with the status of Berlin; the relationship of these German governments, particularly the Federal Republic, to the city was and is complicated and somewhat obscure. The *Grundgesetz* (Basic Law) of the Federal Republic (not called a constitution because that august title is to await the reunification of Germany) listed greater Berlin as one of the twelve *Laender* (states) to which it applied. But the Western military governors, when they approved this basic law, made reservations on Berlin: it was neither to be given voting representation in the federal parliament (though it may and does send non-voting representatives) nor to be governed by the Federal Republic. Likewise, West Berlin's own constitution now describes it as a *Land* of the Federal Republic governed by the latter's *Grundgesetz* and other laws, but the Western Komendatura limited their approval by stipulating that Berlin should have none of the attributes of a *Land* and that the Federal Republic's laws should not apply of their own force to Berlin.

These laws have to be enacted by Berlin's own city government—which, however, can be simply and expeditiously accomplished by a *Mantelgesetz* (cover law) incorporating by reference a law of the Federal Republic or a group of such laws. Under this system Berlin has, in fact, pretty well homologized itself to the Federal Republic in financial and judicial matters: in taxation and public expenditure it is practically a twelfth *Land* of the federation, and it has the same currency. The decisions of its courts are subject to the appellate jurisdiction of those of the Federal Republic. But the *Bundesverfassungsgericht,* the Federation's supreme constitutional court, held in 1957 that so long as the Allied reservations remained in force Berlin was not one of the *Laender* and constitutional questions arising in that city were not within its jurisdiction. The Western Allies were sedulous not to disturb this delicate balance by their 1954 Contractual Agreements (so-called to make sure that nobody confused them with a Peace Treaty) with the Federal Republic. These agreements, though they terminated the occupation in West Germany, changed the mission of Allied forces from occupation to "the defense of the free world, of which Berlin and the Federal Republic form part," and gave the Federal Republic "the full authority of a sovereign state over its internal and external affairs," reserved to the Western powers their rights as military occupants "insofar as they are required for the exercise of the rights" relating to Berlin, Germany as a whole, reunification, and a peace treaty. Passing rapidly over the concept, intelligible only to the *hochgelehrte* among

37

international jurisconsults and not to all of them, that West Germany ceased to be occupied territory but the three Allies continued to be occupants for certain purposes, the intent is tolerably plain—to change radically the relationship between the Western Allies and the West Germans without affecting their status vis-à-vis the Soviet Union. Although Berlin, not being part of the Federal Republic, was not within the scope of these agreements, the Three Powers took the occasion further to increase the control of the city government over its own affairs. But the Allied authorities retained power, *inter alia,* in matters affecting the security of their own forces, the relations of Berlin with authorities abroad, and authority over the Berlin police to the extent necessary to assure the city's security. Moreover, they kept the right to take "such measures as may be required to fulfil their international obligations, to insure public order and to maintain the status and security of Berlin and its economy, trade and communications." As to Berlin, the Western ambassadors continued to be High Commissioners—i.e., military governors—and Berlin continued to be under military occupation. It may well be the only belligerent occupation ever heard of whose prolongation is ardently desired by the inhabitants of the occupied territory.

Parallel subtleties occurred in the East zone. In 1949 a constitution was promulgated for the German Democratic Republic, declaring Berlin to be its capital, although the allocation of powers and duties between the Soviet occupants and the GDR was left undefined, at least by any published document. The Soviet government seems to have followed the Western example in allowing the laws of the GDR to become effective in East Berlin only when adopted by the municipal authorities. In September, 1955, the Soviet signed a treaty with the GDR, allegedly granting it "unrestricted sovereignty." Accompanying letter agreements stipulated that the GDR would exercise "watch and control" over its borders, "the demarcation line between the German Democratic Republic and the German Federal Republic, the outer boundary of Greater Berlin, in Berlin," and the communication lines between the Federal Republic and West Berlin. The tortuous quoted language appears to be intended to emphasize that, while there may be *de facto* boundaries between the GDR, the Federal Republic, and West Berlin, these lines do not exist *de jure*: they are not international borders. But control of the transport of personnel and material of the West Berlin garrisons was "temporarily" reserved to the Soviet High Command "until a corresponding agreement has been reached"—with whom was not stated.

These are the principal facts pertinent to the question of Berlin's status under the law of nations. The main legal questions, as I see them, are these:

What is the source of the rights of the Western Allies? The Soviet Union argues that since the Red Army actually conquered Berlin and is, therefore, its original and sole lawful occupant, Western rights to be there stem from Russian consent and thus depend upon the continued validity of the four-power agreements. The West replies that its rights, though reinforced and confirmed by these agreements, "derive from the total defeat of the Third Reich and the subsequent assumption of supreme authority in Germany"; the right of free access to Berlin, implied as an essential corollary to the right to occupy it, rests on the same basis. Russia, it concludes, cannot retract rights which were not hers to grant or deny in the first place. If the Soviet view were good law, adds the United States (presumably with tongue in cheek), it could adduce Russian violations of the four-power agreements as a ground for their nullification and insist that Saxony and Thuringia, which were conquered by the United States forces, be returned to Western control. The fact seems to be that the Western armies played as important a role in the capture of Berlin as the Red Army did in the conquest of Saxony and Thuringia. Militarily, it is unrealistic to say that any part of Germany was conquered by the particular regiment or division or army or nation which happened first to overrun it.

What is the present status of the agreements providing for Western access to Berlin? The Russian notes of November 27, 1958, denounced the 1944 and 1945 agreements, described above, as "null and void." Are they? These agreements were no doubt intended to be temporary and provisional, from which the Soviet argues that they have expired by their own terms. But this is exceedingly doubtful. The control machinery agreement of November 14, 1944, was to last, if not forever, at least until a central German government had been established and had signed a peace treaty, an event which has certainly not come to pass. Moreover, the protocol of September 14, 1944, the basic agreement on the joint occupation of Berlin, contains no time limitation at all. The Russians argue further that these agreements are merely component parts of the whole structure of four-power agreements for the unification, demilitarization, and general reconstruction of Germany, constituting in effect one big treaty, and that the foundation of this structure has been destroyed by the Western powers' repeated and gross violations of these agreements. International law, like orthodox domestic contract law, does indeed support the proposition that a material breach of a treaty by one of the contracting states, though it does not automatically and instantly terminate that treaty, gives the other party a right to do so—if it acts within a reasonable time and if the first party's failure to perform was not attributable to the complaining party's own wrongful prevention of that performance.[8] If the Soviets' factual premises were correct, the argument that it is entitled to annul the Berlin agreements would have considerable strength, although it would still not meet the fundamental Western argument that the American, British, and French forces occupy Berlin by right of conquest and not by grace of these or any other agreements with the Soviet Union. The difficulty is, of course, that the factual question of which side bears the responsibility for the collapse of quadripartite control and the failure to reach agreement on a permanent settlement is not so easily determined. Both the Western powers and the Soviet Union have done a good many things since 1948 which are hard to square with the language of the original scheme as spelled out

41

in the political and economic principles of the Potsdam Protocol of August 2, 1945, even allowing for the ambiguities of that language. Among the major principles therein agreed upon were, *inter alia,* "the complete disarmament and demilitarization of Germany and the elimination or control of all German industry that could be used for military production"; the "decentralization of the political structure"; and the allowance and encouragement throughout Germany of "democratic political parties with rights of assembly and of public discussion." Each side has turned its zone into a separate economic and political entity, and each has permitted and encouraged its German government to rearm. The Federal Republic clearly corresponds more closely than does the German Democratic Republic to the original conception of the reconstructed Germany. Its political structure, in which the *Laender* have in fact considerable autonomy, is certainly more decentralized than that of the GDR, which is a typical totalitarian state of the Communist variety. The GDR can be said to allow and encourage "all democratic political parties with rights of assembly and of public discussion" only if these words are construed in a highly Pickwickian, or Marxist-Leninist-Stalinist, sense—i.e., by definition a party is not "democratic" if it is not Communist. The Federal Republic acquired armed forces, *eo nomine,* a trifle sooner than the GDR, but the latter's so-called *Volkspolizei* were training with tanks at a time when the Federal Republic had no paramilitary forces more formidable than *Grenzpolizei* armed with rifles and pistols—although, of course, it may be argued that tanks are to be regarded as normal police equipment in most of the Communist states. In short, the foundation of the four-power arrangement for the occupation, control, and reconstruction of Germany was an agreement to agree, and it is notoriously difficult to assess the blame for the failure of such an agreement or even to determine when there has been a failure to bargain in good faith. If, as the West insists (and not without plausibility), it was the Russians whose intransigence first frustrated the consummation of the four-power agreements, the Russians are in no position to cancel any part of that complex of agreements.

The Russians have subsidiary arguments. There is an ancient, rather disreputable principle of international law, dating at least from Roman imperial times, which is summed up in the phrase *"conventio omnis intelligitur rebus sic stantibus,"* the English of which, in very free translation, is that a substantial and material change of circumstances may justify the demand of a party to a treaty to be released from its obligations.[9] It corresponds, of course, to a familiar principle of domestic contract law. If, for example, Germany had agreed as a disarmament measure not to build aircraft factories, and if aircraft lose their military significance, a German government might invoke the doctrine; if such a change in circumstances really had occurred, the other parties to the treaty could not well object. But no such obvious change in circumstances has here taken place; it is hard to see why the presence of the Western forces in Berlin is more onerous for the Russians, or less important to the West, in 1965 than it was in 1945. It is impossible to take seriously the argument that the small Western garrisons constitute a military threat to the Red Army. In any case, even if it is assumed that the principle is tacitly incorporated in every treaty, it seems clear that a party to a treaty cannot normally constitute itself the sole judge of when circumstances have so changed as to bring the clause into play; if it could, there would be an end to a far more important bit of Latinity, *pacta sunt servanda*. Certainly the mere fact that compliance with a treaty has become inconsistent with the expansionist goals of one of the parties has never been considered the kind of change in circumstances which justifies breach of the treaty.

Does the West's right of access include German civilian traffic? The Western Allies say that their rights exist by right of conquest, are those of military occupants, and endure as long as may be necessary for the fulfilment of their responsibilities as occupants. Under Article 43 of the Hague Regulations a military occupant has the duty to "ensure public order and safety," a phrase which includes at least the physical well-being of West Berlin's population and the maintenance of its economy. It probably includes a good deal more, for "public order" is not a very happy translation of the phrase in the French text (which is the controlling text), *"la vie publique."* A better translation might be "normal public life." The Russians do not appear to have contested this interpretation; indeed, the Soviet authorities, simultaneously with the entry of Western forces into Berlin, requested that the latter assume responsibility for the physical care of civilians in the Western sectors. The Russians do object violently to the introduction into the city of "spies, revanchists, and provocateurs," and others bearing choice names from the Marxist *schimpflexikon*. These terms, in this context, seem to refer to the West German politicians who make frequent symbolic visits to West Berlin, which the Federal Republic regards as its real capital.[10] If *vie publique* means normal public life, such political visits seem a reasonable and permissible implementation of the occupant's duty. On the other hand, in the absence of any precedent which is even remotely analogous, it is not crystal-clear that the public order and safety, or even *la vie publique,* of West Berlin require the importation of politicians from the Federal Republic, for this commodity is locally in long supply. At any rate, the view that the Western occupants' responsibilities do entail a right to maintain whatever communications are necessary to the normal life of the population is confirmed by the 1949 agreements ending the blockade. They provided for the removal of all restrictions on communications, transport, and trade between Berlin and the rest of Germany and for the maintenance of that free traffic; they were certainly not limited to the supply of the Western garrisons.

What would be the effect on the West's rights of a peace treaty between the Soviet Union and the GDR? Mr. Khrushchev, stating his legal premise that "it has always been the case that after the signing of a peace treaty the conditions of capitulation lose force in the entire territory which the treaty covers, and throughout this territory the occupation terms are lifted," bounds nimbly to the conclusion that "the occupation rights, of course, would discontinue with the conclusion of a German peace treaty, no matter whether it is signed with both German states or only with the German Democratic Republic, inside whose territory West Berlin lies." This seems to slur over the very substantial distinction between *a* peace treaty and *the* peace treaty. It is certainly true that peace treaties have been an accepted and traditional means of ending belligerent occupations, although there is nothing to prevent such a treaty from providing for a continuance of the occupation. As phrased by Colonel Winthrop, whom the Supreme Court sometimes describes as the Blackstone of military law, "The status of military government (i.e., occupation) continues from the inception of the actual occupation until the invader is expelled by force of arms, or himself abandons his conquest, or till, under a treaty of peace, the country is restored to its original allegiance or becomes incorporated with the domain of the prevailing belligerent."[11] Passing over the question whether either the Soviet or the Western Allies can unilaterally sign a peace treaty with either part of Germany, there is no precedent for the idea that a treaty between one belligerent and the *de facto* government of that part of the conquered territory which it occupies can end the occupation by that belligerent's allies of another part of the conquered territory, particularly when those allies do not recognize the local signatory government. In the past the peace treaty which terminated an occupation has invariably been one between the occupier of a particular territory and a government which the occupier recognized as the lawful sovereign of such territory. The case of the United States on this point, however solidly founded on law, is not much helped by the fact that it signed a separate peace treaty with Japan, as the Russians have not failed to point out on every possible occasion. In fact, however, the Declaration of the United Nations of January 1, 1942, did *not* obligate the United States not to sign a peace with Japan separately from the Soviet Union: it affected only those enemies with which the signatories were then at war, and to Japan Russia was then—and until 1945—a neutral. Moreover, the Russians, though they were uninfluential members of the Allied Control Council in Japan, were not in actual occupation of any part of that country; there was only one Japanese government; and the treaty certainly did not purport to bind the Soviet Union or abrogate such rights as it had.

What is the effect of the "sovereignty" of the German Democratic Republic? The Russians say that after the signing of a peace treaty the GDR will be even more sovereign than it is now. Therefore, since control over air, land, and water communications across its territory is "an inalienable right of any sovereign state," access to West Berlin must, under "generally accepted international norms," depend upon the GDR's consent. I accept as good international law the premise that a sovereign state normally has a right to control its territory. But, even assuming that the GDR is a *de facto*

47

"sovereign state" (only the Communist states recognize it as such *de jure*), the rights of such a state are by no means "inalienable." The territory of a sovereign may be, and often is, subjected to a "state servitude," defined by the late Sir Lawrence Oppenheim as "an exceptional restriction made by treaty on the territorial supremacy of a State by which a part or the whole of its territory is in a limited way made perpetually to serve a certain purpose or interest of another state." [12] The commonest example is a right of transit, and to just such a servitude did the victors in World War II, including the Soviet victor, subject the territory of Germany in the exercise of the supreme authority which they had assumed. Moreover, since state servitudes are "rights *in rem*, they remain valid and may be exercised however the ownership of the territory to which they apply may change." [13] There is, in short, no precedent for the idea that State A, by recognizing a new "sovereign" over territory, can cut off the rights of states B, C, and D to that territory. If, under customary international law or the existing four-power agreements, the territory in question is subjected to such servitude, it is not lifted by the transfer of sovereignty to the GDR any more than A's common law easement to use B's driveway to get to his own house is abolished when B deeds his land to C. It may be a trifle cavalier of A to use the driveway of one whom he is unwilling to meet socially, but it is not illegal. Finally, it should be noted that the blockade-lifting agreements of 1949 speak only of the restrictions imposed by the U.S.S.R., and so might arguably not be directly applicable to a new and different sovereign. But, even if the Soviet Union were willing to rely on so hair-splitting a textual argument, it could not be applied to the original access agreements or to such rights as are inherent in the Western powers' status as occupants.

How about communications between East and West Berlin? Here the U.S.S.R. and the GDR seem to be on firmer ground, at least in so far as the letter of the law is concerned. I find nothing in the four-power agreements that explicitly and unambiguously obligates the Soviet authorities to permit free circulation *within* the city: the agreements refer in terms only to communication between zones and between the zones and Berlin. I note that, although Secretary Rusk's statement of August 13, 1961, described the sealing-off of East from West Berlin as "a violation of the four-power status of Berlin and a flagrant violation of the right of free circulation throughout the city," he did not cite chapter and verse for these rights, whereas he termed the restrictions on travel between East Germany—itself a "zone"—and Berlin a "direct contravention of the four-power agreement reached at Paris on June 20, 1949."[14]

History never repeats itself precisely, and the legal problems arising out of the four-power condominium—if that is the right word—over Berlin have no exact precedents. Nevertheless, accepted international law seems on the whole to justify the conclusions that the Western powers have now, as military occupants, valid rights of access to West Berlin (including access for the purpose of maintaining the normal life of the city) which are reinforced by, but do not depend upon, the four-power agreements; that these agreements cannot be unilaterally abrogated by the Soviet Union; and that these rights cannot be annulled by a treaty to which the Western powers are not parties. This does not mean that no different or better solution can be devised. I hope and believe that in the long run—perhaps I should say the very long run—it will be, although not in all probability along the lines which the parties envisaged, or said they envisaged, in 1944 and 1945. It does mean that such a solution must, as a matter of law, be based on agreement among the states now having rights in Berlin. And perhaps I ought to add that one of those states is the Soviet Union. I have my own ideas concerning the nature of such a solution. That question, however, goes beyond the scope of this paper, and so I shall leave its discussion to my colleagues.

1. The relevant documents up to 1959, which include practically all of those germane to the present problem, are reprinted in UNITED STATES DEPARTMENT OF STATE AND STAFF OF SENATE COMMITTEE ON FOREIGN RELATIONS, 86TH CONG., 1ST SESS., DOCUMENTS ON GERMANY, 1944–1959 (Comm. Print 1959). See also *A Decade of American Foreign Policy: Basic Documents, 1941–1949,* S. Doc. No. 123, 81st Cong., 1st Sess. (1950). An extraordinarily comprehensive collection of documents bearing on Berlin, including statements of the position of the Federal Republic of Germany, and including also some papers of relatively subordinate importance that are not readily available elsewhere, is DOCUMENTS OF THE STATUS OF BERLIN 1944–1959, prepared and edited by the Forschungsinstitut der Deutschen Gesellschaft für Auswärtige Politik under the direction of O. M. von der Gablentz, and published in Munich in 1959. All of the documents therein reprinted are in English.

2. Among the subjects of disagreement in Berlin is the spelling of this Russian term. The original documents spell it "Komendatura"; later ones, such as the Resolution of Representatives of the Allied Commands on the quadripartite allied administration of Berlin of July 7, 1945, spell it "Kommandatura."

3. EISENHOWER, CRUSADE IN EUROPE 396 (1948).

4. See 6 CHURCHILL, THE SECOND WORLD WAR: TRIUMPH AND TRAGEDY 443–52, 522–88 (1954); 1 TRUMAN, MEMOIRS: YEAR OF DECISIONS 60–61, 210–19, 297–304 (1955).

5. See the statement by Ambassador Philip C. Jessup to the UN Security Council, October 6, 1948, 19 DEP'T STATE BULL. 485 (1948); CLAY, DECISION ON GERMANY 25–26 (1950).

6. I have described the creation of the Federal Republic and its relations with the Western Allies in my article on *The "Contractual Agreements" with the Federal Republic of Germany,* 49 AM. J. INT. LAW 125 (1955).

7. See Simpson, *Berlin: Allied Rights and Responsibilities in the Divided City,* 6 INT'L & COMP. L. Q. 83, 98–99 (1957).

8. 1 OPPENHEIM–LAUTERPACHT, INTERNATIONAL LAW § 547 (7th ed. 1948).

9. See *Id.* § 539.

10. See, for example, an exchange of notes between the United States and the Soviet Union in 45 DEP'T STATE BULL. 397, 431, 433, 511, 513 (1961).

11. WINTHROP, MILITARY LAW AND PRECEDENTS 801 (2d. ed. 1920); see Madsen v. Kinsella, 343 U. S. 341 (1952).

12. See generally 1 OPPENHEIM–LAUTERPACHT, *op. cit. supra* note 8 §§ 203–208.

13. *Id.* § 207.

14. N. Y. Times, August 14, 1961, p. 7.

Some Basic Legal Problems
Underlying the Berlin Dispute

HANS W. BAADE*

ON NOVEMBER 27, 1958, the Soviet Union delivered its famous note on Berlin to the governments of the United States, Great Britain, and France, thus terminating a relatively stable if somewhat precarious truce which had prevailed for almost a decade after the Berlin blockade,[1] and once more making Berlin a focal point in the cold war. The Soviet note, and the diplomatic correspondence which it brought forth,[2] gave rise to three basic issues, all connected with the occupation regime for Berlin: (1) the present legality of the occupation of West Berlin (i.e., of the British, French, and United States sectors) by the three West-

* Professor of Law, Duke University. This article was written in April, 1963. Consequently, the author did not have access to several more recent studies. Nevertheless, a re-examination of the text in the light of these later studies led to the conclusion that a substantive revision was not indicated. However, for the sake of completeness and for the convenience of the reader, the references have been brought up to date (October, 1965).

ern occupying powers; (2) the present nature and scope of the right of access of these three occupying powers to their sectors of Berlin via East German land and air space; and (3) the effect of the conclusion of a peace treaty between East Germany and the Soviet Union upon Western Allied rights of presence in, and access to, Berlin.

On August 13, 1961, East German authorities erected the wall between the Western sectors and the Soviet sector of Berlin. East German regulations issued on the same day virtually put an end to the free movement of Germans between the Western sectors and the Eastern sector. While Germans resident in West Berlin could still enter and leave East Berlin without prior permission at one of the authorized crossing points merely by showing their West Berlin identity cards, Germans resident in the Federal Republic henceforth had to procure special entry permits for the Eastern sector. East Germans and East Berliners, on the other hand, had to obtain an exit permit from their local authorities in order to enter West Berlin from East Germany or from the Eastern sector,[3] just as was theretofore required for entry into West Germany.

The actions of August 13, 1961, were directed against Germans, not Western Allies. The same would be the case if East German authorities decided to interfere with passenger and freight traffic by rail, canal, and motor vehicle between West Germany and West Berlin. This traffic has been subject to the control of East German, not Soviet, authorities for some time. The wall and its horrible twin, another blockade, thus raise a completely distinct set of legal problems: (1) Do the Western Allies have a right to: (a) the unrestricted access of West Berliners (and West Germans) to East Berlin; (b) the unrestricted access of East Berliners (and East Germans) to West Berlin; (c) unrestricted German passenger and freight traffic between West Germany and West Berlin? (2) Does the Federal Republic of Germany (i.e., West Germany) have any corresponding rights? (3) If rights under (1) or (2) exist, who is the obligee? (4) How would such rights be affected by the conclusion of a peace treaty between the Soviet Union and East Germany?

A third set of issues, again distinct from the two basic problem areas mentioned above, centers around the substantive contents of the Soviet proposals of and since November 27, 1958. Broadly speaking, these call for the creation of a demilitarized "free city" of West Berlin, the conclusion of a peace treaty with both East Germany and West Germany, and the eventual reunification of Germany through a confederation between the two German states. It seems clear that at least the conclusion of a peace treaty along these lines would require the assent of both German states, i.e., as a practical matter would be subject to the veto of the Federal Republic. But what about plans for a demilitarized free city, especially if coupled with guarantees for access? Could the United States, Great Britain, and France validly conclude such an agreement with the Soviet Union and with East Germany without the concurrence of the Federal Republic? Could they even negotiate along these lines without its authorization? And finally, to what extent could the Federal Republic of Germany negotiate and enter into agreements concerning Berlin with the Soviet Union and with East Germany without the concurrence of the three Western powers?

These would seem to be the three main areas of legal dispute connected with the Berlin problem. They have their roots in three anomalies produced by Germany's transition from World War II to the cold war without an intervening period of peace: the uncertain legal status of Germany, the confused legal status of Berlin, and the enigmatic legal status of Germany's occupation by the four Allied Powers. In the following, an attempt will be made to analyze the first of these three anomalies in more detail,[4] for as will be shown, it lies at the heart of the Berlin dispute.

While it would seem foolhardy to hope that such an investigation can produce many legal solutions of real significance, it is nevertheless hoped that even a descriptive analysis of the various basic legal positions adopted by the main protagonists in the present struggle for Germany will be more conducive to an understanding of the Berlin problem than would be a mere discussion of the claims and counterclaims launched since November, 1958.

The protagonists in the struggle are the United States, Great Britain, France, West Germany, the Soviet Union, and East Germany. As will be seen, the legal positions adopted by the three Western Allies are usually—though not always—identical. They are also generally shared by the Federal Republic, but with some basic and highly significant exceptions. Furthermore, problems of such complexity have produced not only different legal attitudes in point of time but also substantial divergencies between official positions and academic opinion and—in at least some instances—significant differences between the positions taken by the various organs of state even within the same country, e.g., the executive and the judiciary in West Germany. On the other hand, there seems to be an all but complete identity of opinion between the Soviet Union and East Germany, both on the official level and in academic discussion. For this reason, it appears convenient to discuss the legal anomalies of the legal status of Germany by reference to three basic points of view—the West German, the Western Allied, and the Soviet–East German—and to note differences within each of these "camps" where they occur.

The Legal Status of Germany

The basic legal question confronting Germany is whether the German Reich—i.e., the German state which was founded in 1871—still exists as a state, or whether its legal existence came to an end in, or subsequent to, 1945 through: the "unconditional surrender" of the German armed forces on May 7 and 8, 1945;[5] the arrest of the Doenitz government on May 23, 1945;[6] the assumption of "supreme authority with respect to Germany" by the four victorious Allies on June 5, 1945;[7] the breakdown of four-power control machinery in 1948;[8] or the establishment of the Federal Republic of Germany[9] and of the German Democratic Republic[10] in September and October, 1949, respectively.

If the German Reich of 1871 still exists, it will be necessary to determine the relationship of East Germany and West Germany to this state and to each other, and to decide which of these two entities established in 1949—or which other organ—is entitled to act internationally, and to what extent, on behalf of Germany, i.e., of the German Reich. If, on the other hand, Germany ceased to exist as a state, the issue is whether East Germany or West Germany, or both of them, are successor states of the former German Reich and which assets and liabilities passed to which successor state.

The West German Position

Opinion in West Germany, both official and academic, is well-nigh unanimous that the German Reich of 1871 survives as a state. It is argued that the unconditional surrender of the armed forces was nothing more than a military capitulation, and that the armed forces were, in any event, not competent to surrender the sovereignty—and indeed, the very existence—of the state. The arrest of the Doenitz "government" is considered to be totally without significance, as that entity never exercised any real powers. Furthermore, it is contended, the assumption of supreme authority by the Allies did not extinguish the German state, because the Allied declaration of June 5, 1945, specifically states that the assumption of such authority "does not effect the annexation of Germany."[11] The breakdown of central Allied control machinery for Germany is seemingly not regarded as significant by West German authors.

It is generally assumed by West German commentators that the legal prerequisites for the existence of a state are a defined territory, a specific population, and a governmental machinery vested with original powers. However, it is contended, the existence of a state will not come to an end merely because there is a temporary displacement of the governmental machinery. The occupied state continues to exist as a state, and the hiatus of indigenous *suprema potestas* is bridged by the common conscience of the people that their state still exists even if it is presently unable to exercise the attributes of its sovereignty.

The establishment of the Federal Republic of Germany in September, 1949, poses no difficulty for West German adherents of the continuity theory: the Federal Republic was conceived by its founders to be merely a temporary organizational framework for a pre-existing German statehood in the Western-occupied part of Germany, not a new state in its own right. To underline the temporary character of the new constitutional edifice, its constitution was called not *Verfassung* but *Grundgesetz,* i.e., Basic Law instead of constitution. In its very preamble, the Basic Law specifically states that it is enacted only by part of the German people, is merely intended to "provide a new framework for public life in a period of transition," and invites "the entire German people to complete the freedom and unity of Germany in free self-determination." And Article 146 expressly provides that the Basic Law shall be automatically repealed by the coming into force of a constitution adopted by a free decision of the German people.[12]

But what is the relationship between this temporary organizational framework of German statehood and the German Reich itself? After some initial hesitation,[13] the official position of the West German federal government has been that the Federal Republic is "identical" with the German Reich but presently unable to exercise its authority in all of Germany.[14] In more precise terms, this means that the organs of state established by the Basic Law fulfil the functions of corresponding organs of the Reich and that they exercise a sovereign authority which is identical with that of the Reich, but that the territorial scope of the present constitutional order of the Reich is smaller than the territory of the Reich itself, excluding not only East Germany but also the territories beyond the Oder and Neisse which are presently under Soviet and Polish administration.[15]

The "identity theory" is not only the official doctrine of the federal government, but it has also been accepted by the federal Constitutional Court, at least by dictum.[16] It is, however, rejected by a significant portion of academic authors, including the leading commentator on the Basic Law, Professor Klein. The alternative theory advanced primarily by the latter is that the German Reich continues to exist as the common "roof" over both East and West Germany and that the Federal Republic and the German Democratic Republic are "part-states" under this common roof—neither is able to dispose of the rights of the Reich as such without the consent of the other, or of the entire German people.[17]

The basic difference between the identity and the roof theories is that the latter recognizes the German Democratic Republic as a state (to the same extent that it recognizes the Federal Republic as a state) while the former does not. In the view of the government of the Federal Republic, the so-called German Democratic Republic is not a state according to German constitutional law or public international law and therefore is not entitled to represent even part of the German people nationally or internationally.[18]

In official pronouncements, it is usually pointed out in support of this contention: (1) that the German people have not lost the will to unity; (2) that only the government and parliament of the Federal Republic are duly constituted and freely elected; (3) that the East German government not only denies the German people subject to its jurisdiction their right of free self-determination but also exists solely by virtue of the intervention and support of a foreign power, i.e., the Soviet Union. Thus, it is asserted, the East German "state" is illegitimate in origin, illegally created, and lacks the minimum amount of independent effectiveness required by public international law and the general principles of public law.[19] The evidence cited in this connection is quite impressive. Some three million Germans resident in the German Democratic Republic (out of a total population of about twenty million) have come to West Berlin and West Germany between

1950 and August 13, 1961;[20] the uprising of June 17, 1953, was put down only by Soviet intervention.

But, the critics of the identity theory argue, the same observations can be made with respect to several "satellite" states, especially to Hungary since 1956.[21] Is it the contention of the Federal Republic that some or all East European socialist states are not states, or that their governments are not governments? [22] Furthermore, it is pointed out that democratic legitimacy is not a prerequisite for statehood under public international law[23]—nor, it may be added, under general principles of public law. Professor Klein tellingly reveals the weakness of official justifications in support of the identity theory by posing the following hypothetical case: Suppose that by internal political change the Federal Republic becomes a separatist dictatorship, and the German Democratic Republic, an irredentist democracy. Would this political change really destroy the pre-existing legal status of the Federal Republic?[24]

It seems apparent that the component of the identity theory which denies that the German Democratic Republic is a state requires a much more sophisticated justification than is offered by the primarily political pronouncements of the federal government. Authors who attempt such a justification freely admit that democratic legitimation is not a criterion of statehood, that the East European socialist states are states, and that their governments are governments both according to public international law and constitutional theory. But, it is pointed out, the statehood of the East European states as such is not in issue. They are "historic states," and their populations, even if opposed to the present form of government, still are agreed that their countries are separate states. Furthermore, there is only one government in each East European state, whatever its legitimacy. East Germany, on the other hand, was part of the still existing German Reich, at least until 1949. It can become a separate state only if its people acquiesce in separate statehood, not merely in subjection to separate governmental power.[25] Effectiveness of control does not suffice to create new states under general principles of public law; otherwise, a city would be a state. What is required additionally is the reality of the idea of separate statehood, and that, it is argued, is lacking in East Germany.[26]

It is also contended that the international law principle of effectiveness does not operate during belligerent occupation and that the occupant therefore cannot set up a separate state in part of the occupied country.[27] In other words, it is asserted that the creation of states through secession, i.e., separation of a portion of the territory of a pre-existing state, especially under foreign occupation, requires not only effectiveness in the sense of passive obedience but also the will of the subject population to form a separate state. Historical examples of such ultimately unsuccessful outside attempts at carving out new states are Manchukuo, Slovakia, and Croatia.[28]

Even if these arguments are accepted, the "non-existence" component of the identity theory is severely taxed by the recognition actually accorded by various organs of the Federal Republic of Germany to official acts, judgments, and legislation of the German Democratic Republic.[29] There is—or, at any rate, has been—official co-operation even in such matters as the rendition of fugitives from justice.[30] Furthermore, despite the attempts of the federal government to couch its participation in intra-German trade negotiations in private or at most semi-official terms,[31] there seems little doubt that the intra-German trade agreements between East and West Germany are at least closely analogous to international agreements.[32]

Here, it could be answered that in German private international law the application of foreign laws never has depended upon the recognition of foreign states or governments by Germany, but that German courts have always applied, in appropriate cases, the law actually in force at the critical time and place.[33] However, this would not take care of official and semi-official contacts in law enforcement and intra-German trade. The best over-all defense of the non-existence theory against the charge of implied recognition would seem to be that such recognition is of a special character: it relates to things which the Soviet Union could do directly as the occupying power. Thus, the recognition of official acts by East German agencies within this sphere, it can be argued, merely is tantamount to the recognition of delegated acts of the Soviet occupying power;[34] the legality of Soviet occupation of East Germany as such—with all the consequent rights of administration—is not denied by the Federal Republic.[35]

As can be seen, the identity theory, which expresses the official West German view as to the legal status of

Germany, involves a number of assumptions that are highly controversial, even within West Germany itself. Nevertheless, the federal government has strictly adhered to the view that the German Democratic Republic is not a state and has regarded the recognition of East Germany—or, perhaps more accurately, at least the establishing of diplomatic relations with East Germany [36]—by third powers as an unfriendly act constituting an interference in internal German affairs. It broke off diplomatic relations with Yugoslavia when the latter established diplomatic relations with the German Democratic Republic;[37] it seems not unreasonable to assume that a number of uncommitted nations have been deterred by this reaction from following Yugoslavia's lead.[38]

The federal government even would appear to be prepared to take the non-recognition component of the identity theory yet one step further. In the Communist Party case, the Federal Constitutional Court decided that all West German organs of state are under a constitutional duty to seek the reunification of Germany and that they are constitutionally prohibited from taking "actions which obstruct reunification legally or prevent it factually." [39] From this, it has been concluded by some official commentators that the recognition of the German Democratic Republic by the Federal Republic of Germany is constitutionally impossible.[40]

The Views of the Western Allies

While there is no dearth of official West German pronouncements on the legal fate of the German Reich after May 8, 1945, the Western Allies would appear to have approached this question with marked restraint. Nevertheless, none of them completely avoided expressing an official view at some time; on the strength of such materials as are available, it seems reasonable to assume that Great Britain[41] and the United States[42] consider the German Reich still to be in existence, but France does not.[43]

There is even less evidence as to the official United States, British, and French positions with respect to the relationship between the Federal Republic and the German Reich. At the Suez Canal conference held in London in August, 1956, the French representative stated that "the French Government in particular has recognized the German Federal Republic as the legitimate *successor* to the German Empire." [44] A decision of the U.S. Court of Restitution Appeals is squarely in line with the official position of the Federal Republic: "The German Reich remains with another form of Government"—i.e., the Federal Republic.[45] There appears to be no British official communication in point, but an authoritative British treatise on the subject seems to adopt the roof theory.[46] It can thus be said with but slight exaggeration that between them, the three Western Allies manage to adopt every possible alternative view as to the relationship of the Federal Republic to the German Reich.

On the other hand, the Western Allies manifest a unity of viewpoints as to the international legal capacity of the Federal Republic and as to the legal nature of the German Democratic Republic which must seem as puzzling to the international lawyer as it appears plausible to the student of power politics. The Western Allied position is, briefly, that (1) only the Federal Republic can represent the German people in international affairs; that (2) the German Democratic Republic has no legal existence; but that (3) nevertheless the Federal Republic can represent only that part of the German people which is subject to its jurisdiction—i.e., resident in, or otherwise predominantly connected with, the territorial confines of the applicability of the Basic Law.

The exclusive capacity of the Federal Republic to represent Germany internationally was acknowledged by the three Western Allies in a declaration of October 3, 1954, in which they declared:

> They consider the Government of the Federal Republic is the only German Government freely and legitimately constituted and therefore entitled to speak for Germany as the representative of the German people in international affairs.[47]

This declaration was incorporated by reference into the Protocol to the North Atlantic Treaty on the accession of the Federal Republic of Germany[48] and thus constitutes a treaty obligation, not only of the three Western Allies, but of all other NATO members to the Federal Republic of Germany.

But while the Western Allies have thus recognized— and bound themselves to recognize—that *only* the Federal Republic can speak for Germany, they have not committed themselves to the view that the Federal

Republic is competent to act on behalf of *all* Germans, including those resident outside of the Federal Republic. On the contrary, in reply to protests of the federal government in connection with the conventions between France and the Saar,[49] the three High Commissioners stated in a note of August 3, 1951, that "the jurisdiction of the Federal Republic does not extend beyond its territorial limits." [50] This view does not appear to have been superseded by subsequent developments. As recently as on May 23, 1962, for instance, the Department of State sent the following reply to an inquiry regarding the capacity of consular officials of the Federal Republic to act in the United States on behalf of Germans resident in East Germany:[51]

> The question which you raise concerning the capacity of consular officers of the Federal Republic has arisen on a number of occasions in the past and the position of the Department of State has been that consuls of the Federal Republic are not authorized to act on behalf of the German nationals residing in East Germany.[52]

If the Federal Republic is the only sovereign state capable to represent Germany but it cannot act on behalf of East Germans, what is the status of East Germany? The Department of State communication just cited states in this regard:

> The United States does not recognize the regime in Eastern Germany as either a state or a government. The United States considers that the area is under the effective control of the Soviet Union and that the East German regime is but a local instrument of the Soviet Union.[53]

The United States and the two other Western Allies have adhered to this position constantly since 1949, when the German Democratic Republic was established. On October 12 of that year, Secretary of State Dean Acheson stated that "the United States Government considers that the so-called German Democratic Republic established on October 7 in Berlin is without any legal validity or foundation in the popular will." He went on to observe that the new government "was created by Soviet and Communist fiat," that it "rests on no constitution written by democratic representatives" of the states in the Soviet zone, that it "is not the outcome of a free popular mandate," and that despite protestations to the contrary, it is not "free and independent" but "a subservient and controlled government." The Secretary of State concluded:

> Such a government cannot claim by any democratic standard to speak for the German people of the Soviet zone; much less can it claim to speak in the name of Germany as a whole.[54]

On March 25, 1954, the Soviet Union issued a unilateral statement announcing that it was establishing the same relations with the German Democratic Republic as with other sovereign states and that the German Democratic Republic was free to decide on internal and external affairs, including relations with West Germany.[55] A month later, the Allied High Commission announced that the three governments represented in it "do not recognize the sovereignty of the East German regime which is not based on free elections and do not intend to deal with it as a government."[56]

The Western Allied position was reiterated in a joint statement of their foreign ministers on September 28, 1955, after the Soviet Union and East Germany had formalized the relations created by unilateral declaration in 1954 through the conclusion of a bilateral treaty.[57] The three Western foreign ministers thereupon announced that they

> reaffirm that the Federal Republic of Germany is the only German Government freely and legitimately constituted and therefore entitled to speak for Germany as the representative of the German people in international affairs. These three Governments do not recognize the East German régime nor the existence of a state in the Soviet zone.[58]

The three Western Allies have also adhered to this theory of the legal non-existence of the German Democratic Republic and of its government in more recent, direct diplomatic exchanges with the Soviet Union.[59] They have carefully avoided all acts that might be construed as an implied recognition of the East German state or government.

As indicated by the statements quoted above, two arguments are advanced by the Western Allies in support of their theory of "non-existence." The first is that the East German state and government lack democratic legitimacy or, better, legitimation. The second argument—and by far the more weighty—is that the German Democratic Republic is controlled by the Soviet Union to such an extent as to be actually nothing but the *alter ego* of the Soviet occupation authorities. Since it may safely be assumed that neither the

United States, nor Great Britain, nor France would earnestly assert that democratic legitimacy is a precondition for statehood or governmental authority under public international law or by virtue of some ubiquitous notion of public law, the first of these arguments would appear to be—at least as regards its legal connotations—[60] merely a factual assertion in support of the second. For if the East German state and government are not supported by the people, it is all the more plausible to assume that the East German governmental machinery is merely an instrument of the Soviet occupation authorities.

As has been pointed out above, democratic legitimacy —or at least an unequivocal popular decision in favor of separate statehood—is arguably a prerequisite for the creation of a state through *separatio,* or secession.[61] But as the classic example of Austria after 1918 (the "Staat wider Willen") would seem to establish,[62] this prerequisite does not exist where the territory on which the new state is sought to be established is not part of the territory of an existing sovereign state. The official view of the Federal Republic is that East Germany is part of the territory of the still existing German Reich which presently is represented by the organs of the Federal Republic. Consequently, the Federal Republic can maintain, East German statehood can come into existence only through an uncoerced decision of the East German population in favor of separate statehood.[63] But this argument does not appear to be available to the three Western Allies. Since none of them maintain that East Germany is part of a state represented exclusively *and fully* by the Federal Republic,[64] they cannot insist that the more stringent requirements for *separatio* have to be met before a new state can come into existence in East Germany. Consequently, their theory of the non-existence of the German Democratic Republic can rest only upon the proposition that the East German government lacks that degree of indigenous effectiveness which the government of a sovereign state must possess under international law.

Since the termination of vestigial Soviet legal occupation rights in East Germany through the conclusion of a peace treaty between the Soviet Union and East Germany would formally place the German Democratic Republic—at least as against the three Western Allies —in the same category as the other socialist states which are recognized to be sovereign states under international law, the conclusion of such a separate peace treaty poses a serious threat to the legal position of the Western Allies with respect to East Germany. On this issue their position is both stronger and more precarious than that of the Federal Republic. The latter does not regard itself to be bound by the Potsdam Agreement or by any subsequent four-power agreements with respect to Germany not formally assented to by the Federal Republic, and considers all of these *res inter alios acta*.[65] It can therefore only point out as an affected observer but not claim as of right that the Soviet Union is not meeting its four-power obligations with respect to Germany. But the three Western Allies are parties to wartime and postwar agreements with the Soviet Union. While they do assert some rights, especially with respect to Berlin and military access thereto, on the basis of the unconditional surrender of the German armed forces and on military occupation alone,[66] they claim other rights by virtue of agreements concluded with the Soviet Union as one of the powers jointly occupying Germany after World War II. These latter include joint responsibility with respect to Germany, a commitment that "the settlement of the German question and the reunification of Germany by means of free elections shall be carried out in conformity with the national interests of the German people and the interests of European security," [67] the freedom of civilian access to Berlin by land,[68] and possibly some aspects of access to Berlin by air.

It seems somewhat doubtful whether the rights dependent upon obligations assumed by the Soviet Union in its capacity as an occupant of Germany would automatically continue when the Soviet occupation of Germany is terminated. There would, strictly speaking, be no case of state succession, because the Soviet Union is not the territorial sovereign of East Germany.[69] For the same reason, the existence of a state servitude may well be questioned, for ordinarily, the powers which the occupant relinquishes do not survive as such—the occupied country merely recovers, *pro tanto*, its capacity to act. It might even be contended that obligations "in rem" imposed by the occupying power on the occupied state or territory and granted to third states would be *ultra vires* to the extent that they exceed the period of occupation.[70]

For these reasons, the Western Allies have a vital interest in the continuation of Soviet occupation rights (and, of course, duties) in, and with respect to, East

Germany and East Berlin. This basic position was well summarized by Judge Breitel in the Upright case:

> The status of the East German territory is that of territory, once belligerent, but now occupied by a wartime ally, the Soviet Union, with the consent of the other allies. Nonrecognition, in the past, of the East German Government simply meant that, pending a reunification plan and free secret elections, the State Department refused to recognize the displacement of the Soviet Union as the power responsible for the territory and for the conduct of affairs there.[71]

But, of course, there remains the basic question whether the Western Allies are legally entitled to compel the Soviet Union, against its will, to retain occupation rights in, and with respect to, East Germany merely to guarantee the continued existence of Western Allied rights which are contingent upon the existence of a state of military occupation. Furthermore, it might be asked whether in view of the retention of parallel rights by the Western Allies with respect to West Germany, the fact of the occupation of East Germany is any more relevant to the statehood of the German Democratic Republic than the occupation of West Germany[72] is to the international legal capacity of the Federal Republic.

The Soviet and East German Position

In its note of November 27, 1958, to the Federal Republic of Germany, the Soviet government stated that "for nine years two independent states have existed in Germany, both of which enjoy international recognition" and that "the Soviet Union some time ago established the same relationship to the German Democratic Republic and to the German Federal Republic as to other sovereign states."[73] This seems to be an apt summary of the present Soviet and East German position, which is based on the following three propositions: (1) the German Reich has ceased to exist; (2) both the Federal Republic and the German Democratic Republic are its successor states; (3) both of these states are bound by, and entitled to the benefits of, inter-Allied wartime and postwar agreements with respect to Germany.

These views, which have been maintained with regularity by both the Soviet Union[74] and East Germany[75] for about the last ten years, do not appear to have gained official recognition by either government before 1954. Even East German legal literature on the subject of Germany's legal status is amazingly sparse, particularly if compared with the output of West German scholars.[76] Part of this academic reluctance is no doubt due to the relative scarcity of fully qualified socialist legal experts in the formative years of the German Democratic Republic.[77] But it would seem reasonably clear that, until the division of Germany became a relatively long-term political reality in 1954 when the Federal Republic was integrated into the NATO alliance system, both the Soviet Union and the German Democratic Republic studiously avoided expressing any legal views which could become impediments to their political objectives with respect to Germany as a whole.

Nevertheless, practical requirements necessitated at least an answer to the question of the continued legal existence of the German Reich. This became relevant especially in connection with pre-1945 public contract or tort claims against East German political subdivisions.[78] In a landmark decision of October 31, 1951, the East German Supreme Court held that the German Democratic Republic was neither identical with, nor the successor of, the German Reich, and that there was also no relationship of identity or continuity between the respective political subdivisions of these two states.[79]

The court analyzed the problem in the light of both general constitutional doctrine and public international law. With respect to the former, it observed that the essential characteristics of a state are contained in its class structure and in the relationship of the various classes to the instruments of governmental power. Hence, it held, there could be no identity between Hitler's Reich and the German Democratic Republic. But there also could be no succession of the latter into the rights and obligations of the former for "the entire governmental system of the Fascist state was crushed, and the state therefore destroyed, by the Red Army and the Allied troops." The present state was erected from below on the ruins of the old; it is diametrically opposed to the former state in class structure and in public purpose. This state has nothing in common with

Hitler's state, the court concluded, and hence cannot be its successor.[80]

The court then observed that an analysis in the light of public international law would lead to the same result. For in view of Hitler's war aims, his opponents were forced to pursue the goal of destroying this German state which threatened their very existence. In this connection, the court referred to the declarations of Yalta and Potsdam. It concluded that the Allies reached their political objectives on May 8, 1945, and that "unconditional surrender brought an end to the existence of the then existing German state." This did not deprive the German people of their right to reconstitute themselves as a new state, but it did terminate the existence of the German Reich.[81]

In a discussion of this judgment which appeared in the official East German legal periodical, a West German author argued that while the German Democratic Republic was a new state, the Federal Republic was a continuation of the German Reich, especially since the social structures of West Germany and of the Weimar Republic were substantially identical.[82] This view was expressly rejected by the editors, who stated that "in our opinion, the Federal Republic is not a German state organization, but a state organization created by the outside fiat of the Anglo-American imperialists."[83] While again the paucity of legal literature and the dearth of official pronouncements counsel caution in this regard, it seems reasonably clear that the official East German position crystallizing around the 1951

Supreme Court decision was that the German Reich was extinct, that the German Democratic Republic was a completely new state, and that the Federal Republic was not a state but a mere creature of the Western Allied occupation authorities, created in violation of both the form and the substance of Allied agreements relating to Germany.

This view appears to have been quietly abandoned when the Soviet Union, by declaration of March 25, 1954, established "the same relations with the German Democratic Republic as with other sovereign states." [84] East Germany now experienced—and still continues to experience—substantial difficulties in obtaining recognition as a sovereign state. It must have seemed obvious at that juncture that non-socialist states would not be impressed by the argument that the Federal Republic was illegally created in violation of postwar inter-Allied agreements and that only the German Democratic Republic, which lived up to these agreements, was the true German state. Primarily for this reason, it would seem, a now substantially increased stream of East German academic comment was directed toward demonstrating that in accordance with the effectivity test of public international law, the German Democratic Republic is a state.[85] But this argument necessarily assumes that the Federal Republic is a state, too.

Consequently, East German legal commentators have not disputed since 1954 that the Federal Republic is a state. However, they have contended that the Federal Republic is not a *lawful* state: first, because the federal government is claimed to pursue objectives and practices which are incompatible with Allied agreements concerning Germany, especially the Potsdam Agreement; and secondly, because a "monopolistic" capitalist class structure and a bourgeois form of government are asserted to be incompatible with the true interests of the German people as revealed by Marxism-Leninism. Consequently, it is argued, the German Democratic Republic, which meets these tests, is the only *lawful* German state.[86] It is conceded, however, that unlawful as its origins and activities may be, the Federal Republic is also a state, as the effectivity principle of public international law does not make the validity of statehood status contingent upon its legitimacy or legality.[87]

As to the relationship of the two German states to the German Reich, it is now assumed that both are its successors.[88] It is generally agreed in East Germany that the German Reich itself no longer exists, but the time of its extinction is controversial. The apparently dominant view, maintained especially by Professor Kröger, is that the Reich became extinct with unconditional surrender on May 8, 1945.[89] Another view is that this occurred when the four-power administration of Germany broke down; one author prudently limits himself to stating that this issue is presently irrelevant, as the creation of two new states on the territory of a pre-existing state necessarily leads to the extinction of the latter.[90] The 1951 Supreme Court decision, it would appear, is quietly being assigned to oblivion; its holdings as to non-identity and discontinuity, while distinguishable,[91] might yet prove to be embarrassing.[92]

The weakest link in the East German and Soviet argument, it would seem, is that the two German states are bound by Allied wartime and postwar agreements with respect to Germany to which neither the German Reich, nor the Federal Republic, nor yet the German Democratic Republic were parties. To be sure, the latter has expressly accepted the obligations arising out of these agreements. However, it seems doubtful whether this acceptance, which is expressed in unilateral declarations and in a bilateral treaty with the Soviet Union,[93] creates any obligations toward the Western Allies, especially since the absence of Western Allied recognition of the German Democratic Republic as a state precludes reliance and, hence, estoppel. In any event, East German acceptance of Allied agreements with respect to Germany could not bind West Germany.

Here, East German legal authors leave the confines of traditional international law. World War II, they argue, has given rise to a new type of law called "democratic international law." [94] This law, among other things, embodies the outlawry of aggression and of fascism. The Allied wartime and postwar agreements with respect to Germany are, it is argued, mere concretions of this new democratic international law which have found additional sanction in Article 107 of the Charter of the United Nations.[95] Therefore, it is claimed, they are binding upon Germany—and, of course, upon the Allied Powers themselves—not as treaties, but as statements of new rules of general international law.[96]

SOME CONCLUSIONS

The above discussion has shown that there is substantial disagreement as to the legal status of Germany between the main protagonists in the Berlin dispute. The most controversial issues revolve around three questions: the present status of the German Reich of 1871, the relationship of the Federal Republic to the Reich, and the status of the German Democratic Republic. It seems hard to conceive of a solution of the current Berlin question in purely legal terms without a definitive answer to these three questions, especially to the one last mentioned.

Since the identity, continuity, and existence of states is regulated by public international law, one might think that the basic problems underlying the Berlin dispute can be solved by analysis and—if need be— adjudication in terms of international law. But even if we start with the logically irrefutable premise that every dispute is "justiciable," [97] there appears to be little likelihood that an authoritative legal decision of the Berlin problem is within reach.

The main reason for this, it would appear, is not the (quite possibly decreasing) reluctance of the Soviet Union to participate in international adjudication. After all, there are significant and justiciable disputes within the "Western" camp as well; and so fundamental a question as, for instance, the relationship of Berlin to the Federal Republic is not likely to be determined by "intra-Western" adjudicatory processes. Ordinarily, one might think that nothing is more suitable for international adjudication than the West German contention that Berlin is part of the Federal Republic and the Western Allied claim that it is not. But the essential point in issue would be whether the jurisdiction of the Federal Republic in 1949 extended beyond the territory of the then eleven West German states. If it did, Berlin is part of the Federal Republic, but the Federal Republic is prevented by the fact of occupation from exercising its full authority with respect to Berlin.[98] If it did not, the attempt to "incorporate" Berlin into the Federal Republic by appropriate provisions in the Basic Law [99] was an internationally illegal and ineffective attempt at annexation.[100]

A decision in favor of the Federal Republic would cast doubts upon Western Allied assertions that the four-power status of Berlin had been preserved and thus weaken claims to access to Berlin based on agreement with the Soviet Union. It would also give added impetus to the charge of Western aggressive designs, for the Basic Law expressly purports to include not only West Berlin but East Berlin as well.[101] A decision in favor of the Western Allies, on the other hand, would have serious consequences for civilian access to and from Berlin, for any such rights of access not claimed on the basis of miltary occupation but asserted on grounds of practice, servitude, or easement by necessity[102] would then be available only to Berliners, not to West Germans. Above all, however, any judicial decision at all, whichever way it went, would have the most dire political consequences. It would not only weaken the united stand of the Western powers on Berlin by rendering their joint legal assertions less credible, but also raise the specter of the political semi-independence of West Germany under a rudimentary but nevertheless still effective occupation regime.

These latter considerations might be minimized in a straight East-West litigation. However, other obstacles would soon appear. As this paper has shown, every protagonist in the Berlin dispute bases his ultimate argument on several premises—some relatively strong, some rather doubtful, and some possibly futuristic. Consequently, all parties have to fear a reverse on some point. But since all ultimate conclusions are based on deductions drawn from all premises advanced, any such reverse will with some likelihood lead to a total loss of the legal contest.

To be more specific: the Federal Republic might consider its chances of ultimate success to be quite substantial if the identity theory were accepted—but the identity theory is not likely to be accepted.[103] The Western Allies are reasonably sure to prevail on at least some points if the dispute were restricted to the rights and duties of the four occupying powers toward each other, plus the rights of the occupants as such. But again, there is little likelihood that this issue will be considered without reference to the possibility of a unilateral termination of the occupation regime and the consequent lapse of occupation rights in the German Democratic Republic. The Soviet Union and East Germany might be reasonably sure of success on the issue of the statehood of the German Democratic Republic, at least if the identity theory were rejected. But again, the Soviet Union faces the strong possibility of an adverse decision on its assertion of the power to relieve itself by unilateral action from obligations contracted toward the Western Allies.

Thus, all protagonists in the Berlin dispute might be likened to military commanders who are in charge of good fighting machines but each of whom knows that he has at least one weak flank or one major tactical or strategic disadvantage. Under these conditions, no side is willing to risk an all-out battle which might entail total defeat because of a relatively minor weakness, and certainly no commander is so foolhardy as to accept a limited combat on the adversary's own ground. The propagandists of each side cheerfully—and quite possibly even truthfully—say that their center can defeat the enemy's flank, but since this confrontation is rather unlikely, an ordeal by battle (i.e., by international litigation) is studiously avoided. In other words, we have what Lon Fuller has called a "polycentric" dispute: the points in controversy are so interrelated that they cannot be isolated and so complex that the consequences of a "global" adjudication cannot be intelligently foreseen.[104]

Does this mean that international law is of no aid in connection with the Berlin dispute because this dispute is—in Lon Fuller's meaning of the term—not justiciable? One answer might be that the general prohibition of the threat or use of force except for self-defense which is now codified in Article 2, section 4 of the Charter of the United Nations [105] is not only binding

84

on the four Allied protagonists who are members of the United Nations but has also been accepted by both German states.[106] Consequently, general international law imposes at least some significant restraints upon the choice of methods for the solution of the Berlin problem.

This limitation, however, applies to any international dispute at all. Our inquiry here has to be more specific: granted a basic commitment to non-violent international political processes, does the invoking of international law by the protagonists of the Berlin dispute increase or decrease the possibility of a solution? There appear to be some good reasons for answering this question in the affirmative.

First, an argument presented in terms of international law contains the built-in requirement of a minimum degree of consistency. Thus, if the German Democratic Republic argues that by virtue of the effectivity principle of public international law it is a state, it can no longer—and *does* no longer—dispute the statehood of the Federal Republic. If the Western Allies rest their claims in connection with access to Berlin largely on obligations assumed by the Soviet Union in its capacity as the occupation power in East Germany, they are precluded from arguing that the occupation of East Germany by the Soviet Union is unlawful. If, in order to bolster the Western stand, the Federal Republic supports the Western Allied assertions,[107] it too will have to treat the Soviet Union as a lawful occupant of East Germany.[108] Thus, the necessity for logical consistency of legal arguments neutralizes much of the political

85

dynamite of a "liberation" policy—in the East as well as in the West.

Secondly, legal argumentation is inseparably linked to legitimate doubt. Elaborate arguments in legal terms are intended, at least to some extent, to convince others who are receptive to logical argumentation and proof. Consequently, a political argument advanced by a government in legal terms is subject to rational analysis and possible rejection not only abroad but also at home. This may not be so in a socialist state, where the basic tenets of Marxism-Leninism dictate a partisan approach to legal problems.[109] But at least in Western countries, legal scholars can—and do—subject the legal arguments of their own governments to a reasonably unrestrained critical analysis. Politicians and others in public life, on the other hand, can seldom adopt the same critical attitudes toward the basic foreign policies of their governments. It has long been political suicide for a West German politician to argue that the existence of two German states should be recognized. Yet the leading commentary on West German constitutional law has baldly stated—at little risk to its author—that there are two German states.[110] Thus, contrary to the basic charge of the Kennan-Morganthau school,[111] governmental foreign-policy argumentation in legal terms might allow for more freedom of intelligent discussion than would an unabashedly self-interest, power-policy argument.

Finally, even if the states which are parties to a "polycentric" international dispute are unwilling to expose their legal arguments to ordeal by battle in international adjudication, they do not regard their *legal* arguments as non-negotiable. If Germany were politically reunited, the new German state would in all likelihood cheerfully accept any pedigree on which agreement could be obtained. The basic reason for this negotiability is, of course, that legal positions can serve to cover up the real issues, often to the point of distortion.[112] But this is not necessarily a disadvantage. An open clash of unnegotiable power-policy interests will with some likelihood preclude any agreement at all, since the prestige of both sides is all but irrevocably committed.[113] On the other hand, a more rational and restrained, even if artificial, legal disputation will keep the underlying issues open. It will make deadlocks less likely and pose no real obstacles to a political settlement if and when the time is ripe for one. And, of course, there is little doubt that the German question and the Berlin dispute can only be solved by a political settlement.

1. For an excellent analysis of the Berlin blockade, see DAVISON, THE BERLIN BLOCKADE: A STUDY IN COLD WAR POLITICS (1958).

2. Most of the documents referred to in this article are to be found in DOCUMENTS ON THE STATUS OF BERLIN 1944–1959 (VON DER GABLENTZ ed. 1959), [hereinafter cited as VON DER GABLENTZ]; in RUHM VON OPPEN, DOCUMENTS ON GERMANY UNDER OCCUPATION 1945–1954 (1955), [hereinafter cited as RUHM VON OPPEN]; and in *Pinto, Comparative State Practice in International Matters,* 89 JOURNAL DU DROIT INTERNATIONAL CLUNET 1101–39 (1962).

3. Decision of the Council of Ministers of the German Democratic Republic law of August 12, 1961 [1961] 2 GESETZBLATT DER DEUTSCHEN DEMOKRATISCHEN REPUBLIK

332 (Ger. Dem. Rep.). [Hereinafter, East German sources are indicated by an asterisk.]

4. For a discussion of the legal nature of the occupation regime and of the legal position of Berlin, see generally Bishop, *The Origin and Nature of the Rights of the Western Allies in Berlin, supra* p. 23. For legal analysis of the current Berlin dispute, see Wright, *Some Legal Aspects of the Berlin Crisis,* 55 AM. J. INT'L L. 959 (1961); Grewe, *Other Legal Aspects of the Berlin Crisis,* 56 *id.* at 511 (1962); Rauschning, *Die Berlin-Frage im neueren Schrifttum,* 16 EUROPA—ARCHIV 663 (1961); Munich, Berlin 1, WÖRTER-BUCH DES VÖLKERRECHTS 182 (Schlochauer ed. 1960); Schüle, *Berlin als völkerrechtliches Problem,* BERLIN IN VERGANGENHEIT UND GEGENWART 124 (Hans Rothfels ed. 1961); Pinto, *supra* note 2; Green, *The Legal Status of Berlin,* 10 NETHERLANDS INT'L L. REV. 113 (1963); Bathurst, *Legal Aspects of the Berlin Problem,* 38 BRIT. Y.B. INT'L L. 254 (1964); Schulz, *Zu einigen völkerrechtlichen Aspekten der Lösung der Westberlinfrage,* 1964 STAAT UND RECHT* 1770; and Lush, *The Relationship Between Berlin and the Federal Republic of Germany,* 14 INT. & COMP. L. Q. 742 (1965).

5. Act of Military Surrender, May 8, 1945, RUHM VON OPPEN at 28.

6. See LÜDDE-NEURATH, RIGIERUNG DÖNITZS. DIE LETZ-TEN TAGE DES DRITTEN REICHES 45–124 (1951).

7. Declaration regarding the defeat of Germany and the assumption of supreme authority with respect to Germany, RUHM VON OPPEN at 29.

8. For background discussion, see generally DAVISON, *op. cit. supra* note 1; GOTTLIEB, THE GERMAN PEACE SETTLE-MENT AND THE BERLIN CRISIS (1960).

9. See generally GOLAY, THE FOUNDING OF THE FEDERAL REPUBLIC OF GERMANY (1958).

10. See generally DOERNBERG, DIE GEBURT EINES NEUEN DEUTSCHLANDS* (1959); Schultes, *Zur demokratischen Verfassungsentwicklung,* 1950 NEUE JUSTIZ* 2, 39, 76, 186.

11. *Op. cit. supra* note 7, at 30.

12. For a thorough discussion of the legal status of Germany, with copious references to all major sources and docu-

ments, see VON BIEBERSTEIN, ZUM PROBLEM DER VÖLKERRECHTLICHEN ANERKENNUNG DER BEIDEN DEUTSCHEN REGIERUNGEN: EIN BEITRAG ZUR DISKUSSION ÜBER DIE RECHTSLAGE DEUTSCHLANDS (1959); see also SCHUSTER, DEUTSCHLANDS STAATLICHE EXISTENZ IM WIDERSTREIT POLITISCHER UND RECHTLICHER GESICHTSPUNKTE 1945–1963 (1963). Recent English-language literature includes Wengler, *International Law Problems of the Situation of Germany*, 15 REVUE EGYPTIENNE DE DROIT INTERNATIONAL 1, 1959); Pinto, *The International Status of the German Democratic Republic*, 86 JOURNAL DU DROIT INTERNATIONAL (Clunet) 313 (1959); Munich, *The German Problem*, 89 *id.* at 7 (1962); VON GLAHN, THE OCCUPATION OF ENEMY TERRITORY 273–90 (1957); BATHURST and SIMPSON, GERMANY AND THE NORTH ATLANTIC COMMUNITY (1956); and the materials in 1 WORLD POLITY 176–247 (1956).

13. A letter of the Foreign Office to the federal minister of justice dated July 19, 1951, states that "the German State continues to exist and the Federal Republic has to be regarded as identical with the German Reich, or at least as the legal successor of the latter." File no. 512–00–IIIa 9248/51, extract reprinted in 7 DER KONKORDATSPROZESS 119 (Institut für Staatslehre und Politik ed. 1956). But in a letter of July 29, 1954, to the prime minister of Lower Saxony, the federal government stated: "According to unanimous German opinion, which is shared by all political parties of the Bundestag, the Federal Republic is identical with the German Reich." Reprinted *id.* at 89, 90.

14. See, e.g., the official pronouncements reprinted in 18 ZEITSCHRIFT FÜR AUSLÄNDISCHES ÖFFENTLICHES RECHT UND VÖLKERRECHT 733–35 (1958); 20 *id.* at 124–26 (1959).

15. VON BIEBERSTEIN, *op. cit. supra* note 12, at 127–31, especially 129.

16. Concordat case, 6 Entscheidungen des Bundesverfassungsgerichts [hereinafter cited as B. Verf. G.E.] 309, 338 (Ger. Fed. Rep.) (1957). The federal supreme court would appear to have tended toward this position some time before the decision of the Concordat dispute: see 13 Entscheidungen des Bundesgerichtshofs in Zivilisachen [hereinafter cited as B.G.H.Z.] 265, 294–95 (Ger. Fed. Rep.) (1954).

17. VON MANGOLDT, DAS BONNER GRUNDGESETZ 35–38 (2d ed. Klein 1957). See also *id.* at 29–35 for a thorough discussion and documentation of other theories.

89

18. See the official pronouncements cited *supra* note 14. For a political and legal justification of this position, see GREWE, DEUTSCHE AUSSENPOLITIK DER NACHKRIEGSZEIT 138–54 (1960).

19. See, e.g., *ibid.* at 145-46; Grewe, *supra* note 4, at 511; and the sources referred to *supra* note 14.

20. See, e.g., U.S. DEP'T OF STATE, PUB. No. 7256, BACKGROUND BERLIN—1961, at 15 (1961). It should not be overlooked that a sizable portion of the migrants from East to West were primarily motivated by economic and family considerations and that West Germany has, after all, about three times as large a population as East Germany. See VON BIEBERSTEIN, *op. cit. supra* note 12, at 107; and note 160, for a balanced judgment taking these considerations into account.

21. See VALI, RIFT AND REVOLT IN HUNGARY: COMMUNISM VERSUS NATIONALISM (1961).

22. The latter, seemingly absurd assertion has been made by Kordt, *Zur rechtlichen Struktur des Ostblocks,* 1960 JURISTENZEITUNG 553, 56. However, this is not, of course, the position of the federal government.

23. This is conceded by GREWE, *op. cit. supra* note 18, at 142–43. See especially Pinto, *supra* note 12, at 353–61.

24. VON MANGOLDT, *op. cit. supra* note 17, at 33–34.

25. This argument seems to have been advanced for the first time by Fraenkel, *Völkerrecht und Deutsche Demokratische Republik,* 83 DEUTSCHE RUNDSCHAU 1004, 1007–08 (1957).

26. For a thorough exposition of this view, see Stein, *Ist die "Deutsche Demokratische Republik" ein Staat?* 85 ARCHIV DES ÖFFENTLICHEN RECHTS 363 (1961).

27. Munich, *supra* note 12, at 27. See also *infra.* note 28.

28. With respect to Croatia, see United States v. List, 11 Trials of War Criminals 757, 1301–02 (1948). See generally MAREK, IDENTIFY AND CONTINUITY OF STATES IN PUBLIC INTERNATIONAL LAW (1954); LANGER, SEIZURE OF TERRITORY (1947).

29. See, e.g., 20 B.G.H.Z. 323 (1956); 5 B. Verf. G.E. 17, 21 (Ger. Fed. Rep.), (1956).

30. See, Zorn, *Die Entwicklung des sowjetischen Strafrechts und sein Einfluss auf das Recht der Sowjetzone,* [1957] GOLDTAMMERS ARCHIV 108, 114–16. *Cf.,* however, 11 B. Ver. F. G. E. 150 (1960) and 12 B. Ver. F. G. E. 99 (1961), holding that the execution of politically motivated East German judgments in penal matters in West Germany is unconstitutional; Doehring, *Die Teilung Deutschlands als Problem der Strafrechtsanwendung,* 4 DER STAAT 259 (1965).

31. For details, see VON BIEBERSTEIN, *op. cit. supra* note 12, at 203–04.

32. See generally Joetze, *The Legal Nature of Trade Agreements between West and East Germany,* 16 YEARBOOK OF WORLD AFFAIRS 172 (1962).

33. See, e.g., the sources collected in BAADE, DAS VERHÄLTNIS VON PARLAMENT UND REGIERUNG IM BEREICH DER AUSWÄRTIGEN GEWALT DER BUNDESREPUBLIK DEUTSCHLAND 101–02 n. 67 (1962). The contrary assertion with respect to "practice in civil law states" in RESTATEMENT, FOREIGN RELATIONS LAW, Reporter's Note 116 (Tent. Draft 1962) would appear to be in need of drastic re-examination.

34. See generally SCHEUER, DIE RECHTSLAGE DES GETEILTEN DEUTSCHLAND (1960).

35. However, the Federal Republic places increasing emphasis upon the right of self-determination of the German people under general international law and on the corresponding obligation of the Soviet Union to permit the whole German people to decide upon the form of government in Germany. See the statements of the foreign minister of November 29, 1956, the memorandum of the federal government of September 7, 1956, and the statement of the permanent secretary of the Foreign Office of September 28, 1956, reprinted in excerpt in 18 ZEITSCHRIFT FÜR AUSLÄNDISCHES ÖFFENTLICHES RECHT UND VÖLKERRECHT 705–07 (1958). Furthermore, the federal government has called to the attention of the Soviet Union that the latter is, pursuant to four-power agreements relating to Germany, charged with responsibility for the reunification of Germany. Note of January 5, 1959, VON DER GABLENTZ at 217, 24–25.

36. It has been pointed out that a number of Asian and African states probably recognize the German Democratic Republic as a state but are unwilling, for political reasons, to establish diplomatic relations with it because they do not wish to disturb their friendly relations with the Federal Republic or to place additional obstacles in the path of German reunification. See VON BIEBERSTEIN, *op. cit. supra* note 12, at 74 n. 25, 76 n. 32, 219–22.; Misra, *Recognition of the G.D.R.—An Appraisal of India's Policy,* 1963 INDIAN Y.B. INT'L AFFAIRS 116.

37. See the note of the federal government of October 15, 1957, to the government of Yugoslavia, reprinted in extract in 20 ZEITSCHRIFT FÜR AUSLÄNDISCHES ÖFFENTLICHES RECHT UND VÖLKERRECHT 93–94, with further references *id.* nn.16–19.

38. *Cf.* GREWE, *op. cit. supra* note 18, at 155–60; 161–63.

39. 5 B. Verf. G.E. 85, 128 (1956).

40. Rumpf, *Verhandlungen mit Pankow auch rechtlich unmöglich,* [1958] BULLETIN DES PRESSE- UND INFORMATIONSAMTES DER BUNDERSREGIERUNG 481, especially 483. *Cf.* GREWE, *op. cit. supra* note 18, at 143. Such views have been adversely criticized by Menzel, *Falsche staats- und völkerrechtliche Thesen zur Wiedervereinigung,* [1959] BLÄTTER FÜR DEUTSCHE UND INTERNATIONALE POLITIK 707, and by BAADE, *op. cit. supra* note 33, at 111 n. 88.

41. In R. v. Bottrill *ex parte* Keuchenmeister, [1946] 1 A11 E.R. 635, 636 (K.B.), the Court had before it, and gave effect to, a certificate from the secretary of state for foreign affairs which stated, *inter alia,* that in consequence of the Allied declaration of June 5, 1945, "Germany still exists as a state and German nationality as a nationality, but the Allied Control Commission are the agency through which the government of Germany is carried on."

42. The only authorities in point which could be located are decisions of the Court of Restitution Appeals, a United States court of the Allied High Commission for Germany. Kaufmann v. Deutsches Reich, 1 Court of Restitution Appeals Reports 463, 468–73 (1951); Hockenheimer v. Deutsches Reich, 2 *id.* at 234 (1951); Fisch v. Deutsches Reich, *id.* at 534 (1951).

43. The chief prosecutor of the French Republic before the International Military Tribunal at Nuremberg stated on January 17, 1946, that "in the present situation there is no German state." 5 INTERNATIONAL MILITARY TRIBUNAL, TRIAL OF THE MAJOR WAR CRIMINALS 389.

44. U. S. DEP'T OF STATE, PUB. No. 6392, THE SUEZ CANAL PROBLEM 62, 63 (1956), emphasis added. He also stated, however, that "we cannot doubt that the German Federal Republic is the legitimate *representative* of the *ex*-German Empire." *Id.* at 64, emphasis added.

45. Kaufmann v. Deutsches Reich, *supra* note 42, at 473.

46. BATHURST and SIMPSON, *op. cit.*, *supra* note 12, at 184–95, especially 194.

47. Final Act of the Nine Power Conference held at London, September 28 to October 3, 1954, Part V, RUHM VON OPPEN at 600, 606, 607.

48. Protocol to the North Atlantic Treaty on the Accession of the Federal Republic of Germany, preamble, third paragraph. 6 U.S.T. (pt. 5) 5707, 08.

49. Of March 3, 1950, RUHM VON OPPEN at 469-83 (French texts).

50. French text in DOCUMENTS ON INTERNATIONAL AFFAIRS 1951, at 247, 248 (Folliot ed. 1951).

51. There is even at the present only one German nationality; and the Federal Republic asserts that it is authorized to protect all German nationals abroad. SCHÄTZEL, DAS DEUTSCHE STAATSANGEHÖRIGKEITSRECHT 83 (2d ed. 1958). However, it must now be doubted whether this last remaining legal link between the two Germanies can long continue to stand the test of time. A recent article by Riege, *Staatsbürgerschaft und nationale Frage*, 1964 STAAT UND RECHT* 56, has substantially added to already existing apprehensions on this score.

52. Reprinted in Bilder *et al., Contemporary Practice of the United States Relating to International Law*, 57 AM. J. INT'L L. 403, 410 (1963).

53. *Ibid.*

54. RUHM VON OPPEN at 424.

55. *Id.* at 597.

56. Von der Garlentz at 160, 161.

57. Treaty on Relations between the German Democratic Republic and the U.S.S.R. of September 20, 1955, art. 1, [1955] 1 Gesetzblatt der Deutschen Demokratischen Republik* 917, 918.

58. Von der Gablentz at 167.

59. See, e.g., the United States note of July 17, 1961, to the Soviet Union, in U.S. Dep't of State, *op. cit. supra* note 20, at 31, 33.

60. It is, of course, of eminent political significance in the cold war context. See especially Grewe, *op. cit. supra* note 18, at 138–54, and for an entirely different viewpoint, Neal, War and Peace in Germany (1962).

61. *Supra* at p. 63.

62. See Adamovich, Handbuch des österreichischen Verfassungsrechts 22, 23 and n. 1 (5th ed. Spanner 1957).

63. *Supra* at p. 63.

64. *Supra* at pp. 67–68.

65. Note of January 5, 1959, to the Soviet Union, Von der Gablentz at 217, 220–21. See also the statement of the representative of the federal government, Professor Kaufmann, in the Communist Party trial before the federal Constitutional Court on December 7, 1954. Professor Kaufmann would appear to have earnestly contended that (1) reliance of the federal government on the Potsdam Agreement would be an internationally illegal invasion of the *domestic jurisdiction* [*sic*] of the signatory powers; and that (2) the examination of the validity *or meaning* [*sic*] of a treaty between third powers by a German court would likewise be violative of international law for the same reason. 1 Pfeiffer and Strickert, KPD–Prozess 233–34 (1955). The court left the question of the applicability of the Potsdam Agreement under internal German law or under public international law expressly open, 5 B. Verf. G.E. 85, 117, 121 (1956), but only because the Agreement, *as interpreted by the court,* proved to be inconclusive with respect to the issues to be decided. *Id.* at 112-21.

94

66. See, e.g., the United States note of December 31, 1958, 40 Dep't State Bull. 79 (1959).

67. Directive of the four heads of government to their foreign ministers at the Geneva Summit Conference of July, 1955, cited as evidence of Soviet acknowledgment of the obligation to maintain the unity of Germany in the United States note of July 17, 1961, in U.S. Dep't of State, *op. cit. supra* note 59, at 33.

68. So-called Jessup-Malik agreement of May 4, 1949, terminating the Berlin blockade and counterblockade; text in Von der Gablentz at 95. For background, see Davison, *op. cit. supra* note 1, at 254–80.

69. This is brought out by Rauschning, *supra* note 4, at 666–67, but it is seemingly overlooked by Wright, *supra* note 4, at 963. See generally Von Glahn, *op. cit. supra* note 12, at 257–61; Greenspan, The Modern Law of Land Warfare 604–08 (1959).

70. Greenspan, *op. cit. supra* note 69, at 607. See also Note, *Problem of State Succession in Africa: Statement of the Prime Minister of Tanganyika,* 11 Int'l. & Comp. L. Q. 1210 (1962), for the assertion that privileges granted to third states by the Mandatory or Trustee power do not survive the independence of the mandate or trusteeship territory —seemingly a persuasively analogous case.

71. Upright v. Mercury Business Machines Co., 13 App. Div. 36, 42, 213 N.Y.S.2d 417, 423 (1st Dep't 1961). See also the certificate of the British Secretary of State for Foreign Affairs of November 6, 1964, in response to an inquiry by the Court of Appeal in the Zeiss case: "Since [June, 1945] and up to the present date Her Majesty's Government have recognised the State and Government of the Union of Soviet Socialist Republics as de jure entitled to exercise governing authority in respect of [East Germany]. In matters affecting Germany as a whole, the States and Governments of the French Republic, the United Kingdom of Great Britain and Northern Ireland, the United States of America and the Union of Soviet Socialist Republics were jointly entitled to exercise governing authority. . . . In the period from August 30, 1945, to March 20, 1948, they did exercise such joint authority through the Control Council for Ger-

many. Apart from the States, Governments and Control Council aforementioned, Her Majesty's Government have not recognized de jure or de facto any other authority purporting to exercise governing authority in or in respect of that zone." Carl Zeiss Stiftung v. Rayner & Keeler Ltd. (No. 2), [1965] 2 W.L.R. 227, 285 (C.A.).

72. For a brief discussion of the various phases of the occupation of Germany by the United States, see Best v. United States, 292 F.2d 274 (Ct. Cl. 1961).

73. VON DER GABLENTZ at 189, 191.

74. See, e.g., the statement of the Soviet representative at the London Suez Canal conference, *op. cit. supra* note 44, at 58, 59. This statement prompted the French reply quoted *supra* note 44.

75. See, e.g., the verbal notes of the German Democratic Republic of February 21, 1956, to Sweden, and of April 17, 1957, to Austria, 1 DEUTSCHE AUSSENPOLITIK* 280 (1956) and 1 *id.* at 520 (1957).

76. Rolf Stödter, Deutschlands Rechtslage, which appeared in 1948, already lists voluminous German literature on this subject in the bibliography. *Id.* at 275–86.

77. For a sharply critical appraisal of the legal profession in East Germany, see Cohn, *German Legal Science Today,* 2 INT. & COMP. L. Q. 169, 69–78 (1953).

78. See generally Abendroth, *Die Haftung des Reiches, Preussens, der Mark Brandenburg und der Gebietskörperschaften des öffentlichen Rechts für Verbindlichkeiten, die vor der Kapitulation vom 8. 5 1945 entstanden sind,* 1947, NEUE JUSTIZ* 468.

79. 1952 NEUE JUSTIZ* 222 = 1 Entscheidungen des Obertsen Gerichts in Zivilisachen* 241 (1951). The same conclusion had been reached by the Oberlandesgericht Schwerin in a decision of June 18, 1951, NEUE JUSTIZ* 468.

80. 1952 NEUE JUSTIZ* 223.

81. *Id.* at 223–24.

82. Beyer, *Zum gegenwärtigen völkerrechtlichen Status Deutschlands,* 1952 NEUE JUSTIZ* 535, 537.

83. *Id.* at 535.

84. *Op. cit. supra* note 55.

85. Peck, Zum völkerrechtlichen Status der Deutschen Demokratischen Republik* 10–20 (1956); Martin, *Es gibt zwei deutsche Staaten,* 2 Deutsche Aussenpolitik* 834, 839–40 (1957); Kröger, *Adenauers "Identitätstheorie" und die völkerrechtliche Stellung der Deutschen Demokratischen Republik,* id. at 353, 362–63.

86. E.g., Kröger, *Die Deutsche Demokratische Republik—der rechtmässige deutsche Staat unde legitime Vertreter des deutschen Volkes,* in: Staat und Recht im Lichte des Grossen Oktober* 121 (1957); Kröger, *Die staatsrechtliche Bedeutung des Potsdamer Abkommens für das deutsche Volk,* Festschrift für Erwin Jacobi* 197, 220–25 (1957). See also Schirmer, *Zur Völkerrechtssubjektivität der Staaten und zum Problem ihrer völkerrechtlichen Rechtmässigkeit,* 1963 Staat und Recht* 647.

87. See, e.g., Peck, *op. cit. supra* note 85, at 7; Martin, *supra* note 85, at 843; Kohl, *Mehrstaatlichkeit Deutschlands und Wiedervereinigung* 1957 Staat und Recht* 843, 846–47; and especially Schirmer, *supra* note 86.

88. See, e.g., the notes cited *supra* note 75; Brandweiner, *Die Deutsche Demokratische Republik und das Problem der Staatennachfolge,* 1 Deutsche Aussenpolitik* 497 (1956).

89. Kröger, *supra* note 86, at 199–209.

90. Compare Martin, *supra* note 85, at 841, with Peck, *op. cit. supra* note 85, at 7.

91. The case concerned contract claims of an architect against an East German municipality arising out of contractual relations entered into before May 8, 1945. The court referred to the extinction of the German Reich as a subject of international law merely to bolster its prior conclusion that as a matter of German constitutional law, there was no identity of organs or succession as to obligations. Thus, it would appear that there was no ruling—and possibly not even a *dictum*—as to state succession in the international sphere. See 1952 Neue Justiz* 223–24.

92. Especially when political subdivisions of the German Democratic Republic claim, by virtue of state succession or some kindred title, public property situated in the Federal Republic. This is not so far-fetched, as the Iron Curtain did not invariably follow the political boundaries of the German states and provinces existing in 1945. For an illustrative case, see the decision of the Oberlandesgericht Schleswig of March

97

14, 1958, [1958] Recht in Ost und West 168, aff'd by the Bundesgerichtschof, February 17, 1961, [1961] *id.* at 209, recognizing that valid title had been conferred to the beneficiary of a Mecklenburg agrarian reform of September 5, 1945, with respect to land now situated on the "Western" side of the Iron Curtain and for all practical purposes incorporated into Schleswig-Holstein.

93. The treaty of September 20, 1955, *supra* note 57, states in its preamble that it was concluded, *inter alia,* "with due regard being given to the obligations of the German Democratic Republic and of the Soviet Union pursuant to agreements concerning Germany as a whole." A letter of the East German foreign minister of September 20, 1955, to the Soviet deputy foreign minister confirmed a simultaneous agreement that "for the time being," control over the movement of Western Allied military personnel and equipment to and from Berlin would remain in Soviet hands. Von der Gablentz at 166.

94. See especially Kröger, *Das demokratische Völkerrecht und die Grundlagen der Bonner "Hallstein-Doktrin,"* 1961 Staat und Recht* 963, 1187, 1194 ff.

95. U.N. Charter art. 107 provides: "Nothing in the present Charter shall invalidate or preclude action, in relation to any state which during the Second World War has been an enemy of any signatory to the present Charter, taken or authorized as a result of that war by the Governments having responsibility for such action."

96. Schirmer, *supra* note 86, at 657–58.

97. That is, so long as a claim not supported by law will be rejected and a decision in favor of defendant is at least to some extent *res judicata.* See Kelsen, Principles of International Law 383; Menzel, Völkerrecht 327–28 (1962).

98. This is the dominant West German thesis, approved by the federal Constitutional Court, 7 B. Verf, G.E. 1, 7–13 (1957). See generally Drath, *Die staatsrechtliche Stellung Berlins,* 82 Archiv des öffentlichen Rechts 27 (1957); Kreutzer, *West Berlin: City and State,* in Berlin—Pivot of German Destiny 67–99 (Robson ed. 1960).

99. Especially article 23 which refers to "Gross-Berlin" as a state of the Federal Republic. For commentary, see Von Mangoldt, *op. cit. supra* note 17, at 646–50.

100. For a statement of the Western Allied position, see PLISCHKE, BERLIN: DEVELOPMENT OF ITS GOVERNMENT AND ADMINISTRATION 111–34 (1952) ; and especially Lush, *supra* note 4. See also the decision of the U.S. Court of Appeals of the High Commission for Germany in Hartje v. Yugoslav Military Mission, 20 Court of Appeals Reports 197, 201 (1954) : "It is clear that the Federal Republic of Germany has no governmental authority over Berlin and that the Allied Control Authority, the Allied Kommandantura and the City Council and Senate are the only governing bodies in Berlin. Accordingly, the fact that Yugoslavia has an embassy accredited to the Federal Republic of Germany can have no bearing upon the functions and status of its military mission in Berlin which is accredited to another independent governmental authority and territory." (Footnotes omitted). So far as can be determined, the only West German author who shares this view is Schüle, *supra* note 4, at 132–33.

101. Cf. *supra* note 99; see especially Kröger, *Zu einigen Fragen des staatsrechtlichen Status von Berlin,* 3 DEUTSCHE AUSSENPOLITIK* 10 (1958).

102. In the Right of Passage Over Indian Territory case [1960] I.C.J. Rep. 6, Portugal contended, *inter alia,* that its right of access to the enclaves surrounded by Indian territory existed by virtue of a principle of law recognized by civilized nations. *Id.* at 11–12. In support of this contention, Portugal submitted to the court an opinion on "The Law Concerning Ways of Necessity," prepared by Professor Max Rheinstein of the University of Chicago Law School. 1 CASE CONCERNING RIGHT OF PASSAGE OVER INDIAN TERRITORY—PLEADINGS 714–27 (I.C.J. 1960). The court did not decide this question. See, however, the dissenting opinion of Judge *ad hoc* Fernandez [1960] I.C.J. Rep. 123, 136.

103. See *supra* at pp. 61–65.

104. Fuller, *Adjudication and the Rule of Law,* 1960 Proceedings, AM. SOC. INT'L L. 1 ; Fuller, *Collective Bargaining and the Arbitrator,* 1963 WISC. L. REV. 3, especially 31–35.

105. U.N. CHARTER art. 2, sec. 4 provides : "All Members shall refrain in their international relations from the threat or use of force against the territorial integrity or political independence of any state, or in any other manner inconsistent with the Purposes of the United Nations."

106. The declaration of the federal government of October 3, 1954, states: "The Federal Republic has agreed to conduct its policy in accordance with the principles of the Charter of the United Nations and accepts the obligations set forth in Article 2 of the Charter." Article 2, section 1 of the Soviet–East Germany treaty of September 20, 1955, provides: "The Contracting Parties announce their readiness to participate in the spirit of sincere cooperation in international actions designed to safeguard peace in Europe and in the whole world, and which are in accordance with the Charter of the United Nations." *Op. cit. supra* note 57.

107. Note of January 5, 1959, to the Soviet Union, VON DER GABLENTZ at 217: "The Federal Government furthermore shares the view that the Soviet Government is not entitled·to transfer to authorities of the so-called G.D.R., the powers held by it under occupation law and relating to the presence of Western armed forces in Berlin and to the freedom of access to that city."

108. However, the recognition of the legality of the continued Soviet occupation of East Germany is seemingly not incompatible with the assertion that the Soviet Union is obliged, both under international agreements and by general international law, to pursue the policy of the eventual reunification of Germany through the free self-determination of the German people: see *supra* note 35.

109. *Cf.* Baade, *Book Review,* 11 AM. J. COMP. L. 464–65 (1962).

110. VON MANGOLDT, *op. cit. supra* note 17.

111. E.g., KENNAN, AMERICAN DIPLOMACY 1900–1950, at 95–103 (1952).

112. See generally Mendlovitz, *A Relevant Legal Context for the Problem of West Berlin, infra* p. 101.

113. See NICOLSON, THE EVOLUTION OF DIPLOMATIC METHOD 72–93 (1954); LIPPMANN, THE PUBLIC PHILOSOPHY 11–60 (1955). A pioneering study of this aspect of "open" diplomacy is Friedrich, *Die Problematik der Willensbildung in der äusseren Politik,* 22 ZEITSCHRIFT FÜR POLITIK 645 (1933).

A Relevant Legal Context for the Problem of West Berlin

SAUL MENDLOVITZ*

SOME TIME AGO, while preparing this paper, I attended a conference entitled "Berlin: Wall or Bridge?"[1] The following summary is an injustice to the richness of the analyses of the panelists[2] and the ensuing discussion, but in the main, the following framework evolved. The wall is a terrible thing; however, the issues it raises are not novel but part of the issues of the cold war. Berlin is a crucial area because here the superpowers confront each other directly with their armed forces. Whether Berlin is a symptom or a symbol of cold war tensions, has independent military value, or is a potential area for concentrated subversive activity, no solution of the "Berlin Problem" is possible without a good deal of attention to European and Soviet security. Furthermore, the medium-sized states

* Professor of Law, Rutgers University Law School. The author wishes gratefully to acknowledge the extensive and painstaking research aid and editorial assistance of Miss Barbara A. Kulzer in the preparation of this article.

of both Western and Eastern Europe have during the past five years undergone significant, if not radical, transformation in economic and social organization and important political changes in their relationships to the superpowers; no solution will be viable unless it comprehends these changes.

The preferred solutions of the panelists tended toward a disarmed united Germany with proper security measures for both East and West, but since such an "over-all" settlement was generally agreed to be politically unfeasible, more "modest proposals" were suggested. Recognition of East Germany in exchange for guaranteed security of West Berlin or a three-German solution, perhaps with no formal recognition of East Germany and again with a guaranteed security for West Berlin, were offered as realistic, both in terms of security and of moving away from a situation clearly dangerous to world peace. In the spectrum of positions on Berlin and Germany, these solutions might be labeled as hard-headed, left-of-center.[3] Although they deserve serious consideration, my purpose in presenting them here is not to examine their feasibility but to provide a setting for the subject matter of this essay. In the formal presentation of the panelists and in a day of spirited and relevant discussion, international law and international organization were given almost no consideration in the set of problems and solutions being investigated.[4] Impressed by this absence, I asked the panel: What relevance, if any, do international law and international organization (especially the United Nations) have to the events and questions surrounding Berlin? To what extent might they have relevance? To what extent should they?

Again over-summarizing their remarks, I think it can be fairly said that all the panelists agreed that neither international law nor the United Nations had been a significant factor, nor were they likely to be. There was some expression of the classic ambivalence about the use of international law and organization in such matters as Berlin. On the one hand, there was the attitude that it was a pity that more attention was not devoted to the use of international law; certainly, we should give a good deal more attention to the potential role of the United Nations. On the other hand, the members of the panel were quick to warn that a "legalistic" view of these matters tended, at best, to be obfuscating and, at worst, impeded serious investigation of underlying issues and probably obstructed fruitful negotiations.[5]

Perhaps such answers are not disturbing to the reader, and the true professional in the field of international law would have dismissed the incident and gone about his business of phrasing legal problems and solving them. It occurred to me, however, that since such attitudes are relatively typical of many people in connection with the role of law in international affairs, even the true professional might want to consider the merits of these propositions. And so the question: What is the relevance of the legal context to the solution of the Berlin problem?

Let me initiate an answer to this obviously composite question with a concrete example. Several United

States senators, reporting on a trip to Germany in December, 1962, noted that

> Russian military forces have access to the Western sector and Allied military personnel have access to the Eastern sector. Russian soldiers still enter the Western sector regularly to share in the guard over German Nazi war criminals in Spandau prison. They enter, too, to guard the Russian war memorial and to cooperate in the Berlin Air Safety Center.
>
> U.S. civilian officials no longer travel by automobile into the Eastern sector, but do so by U- or S-bahn. They have forgone entering East Berlin by vehicle in order to avoid submitting identification to the East German guards at the checkpoints. Russian civilian officials, on the other hand, do enter the Western sector, identifying themselves, not to West Germans, but to Western military officials who still control the checkpoints.
>
> This irritating disparity in which Russian officials move with relative ease in the Western sector but the reverse does not apply grows out of a legalistic dilemma. For the Western nations to cut off access to Russian officials would be to suggest that the Russians can legally terminate Western access to the Eastern sector. To install Germans in positions of final authority to check the credentials of Russian civilian officials entering the zone would be to acknowledge that what the Russians have done with respect to their zone is legally permissible. Either way, the effect of Western retaliation would be to strengthen the legality of the Russian actions in East Berlin. Either way the effect would be to strengthen the Communist concept of a divided Berlin in a divided Germany.
>
> The issue has not yet arisen with regard to Western military personnel. The East German guards wave them into the Eastern sector without chal-

lenge, contending that they have been identified on the strength of their uniforms. Similarly, as noted, while there has been control over the nature of Russian military movement into and within West Berlin, the legal right of the Russians to enter has not been denied.[6]

If the question of the relevance of legal context is translated to some operation permitting us to measure the instances where international law norms may be said to have been determinative in some appreciable social behavior, then it must be acknowledged that from the erection of the wall [7] until the present time, United States officials within Berlin, at a point of direct contact with the Soviet Union, have used international law norms to guide their behavior. This behavior has involved some inconvenience, petty irritation, and inhibition of normal impulse to retaliate. It should be noted and emphasized that to have used other guidelines, resulting in other behavior (such as retaliation in kind), need not have meant an outbreak of hostilities or even a diminution in the capacity to defend West Berlin. According to the senators' report, this policy was followed in order to abide by the law and to maintain the legal position of the United States.

Two "legalistic" aspects of the situation reported by the senators should be noted. First, the United States is concerned that no actions taken by its officials be understood as "recognition" of East Germany, not only as a government, but as a state.[8] This assumes that there is a generally understood area of international law dealing with recognition [9] and that certain actions, even if accompanied by disclaimers, would be interpreted as recognition by other states.[10] The Soviet Union and East Germany would thus be provided with additional facts and arguments for the position that East Germany is a state within the full meaning of that word in international law. This matter of recognition, it should be observed, is not something arising out of the particular events of Berlin but arises out of the fundamental fabric of international law.[11] Second, the United States feels that certain Russian actions are violative of agreements concerning Berlin [12] but is concerned that these objections should not be considered waived or the agreements invalidated by any Western action contrary to their terms. While this course of activity also applies to the recognition problem, it is distinct in that it is influenced by the terms of quadripartite agreements.

Viewed from the perspective of the sources of international law, then, the course of activity noted in the senators' report indicates that custom, treaties, and publicists' writings are still considered as sufficiently important and persuasive enough to influence Western behavior according to the specific rules emanating from them. To what extent there is some correlation between the various sources of international law and those instances where international law may be said to have had an impact has yet to be explored in any systematic fashion. Perhaps this would not be a useful way of investigating under what circumstances and in what ways international law norms affect behavior. But it can hardly be denied that in this particular instance such norms are operating to affect behavior, and the norms come from a wide range of traditional authoritative sources.

Aside from the obvious caveat that this is but one instance of the relevance of law to Berlin, there is also the serious problem of causality—shared, it might be noted, with all those social sciences dealing with the relationship of norms to behavior. Whether the use of legal norms is a product of other social forces and the determination of the nature of the operation of such norms are questions which might legitimately be explored. Even if the causality problem is bypassed, the methodological difficulties of determining whether law has been a significant influence upon behavior are formidable. What units of behavior in the universe of social events are to be studied? What will be the operational test for impacted behavior (behavior influenced by international law norms)? Specifically, for purposes of discovering the relevance of a legal context to a solution for Berlin, what is the impact of law in an instance where the law is in dispute?

For example, Quincy Wright has assumed that the erection of the Berlin wall was legal.[13] Certainly the Warsaw Pact members take this position.[14] The NATO states, of course, declare it to be illegal.[15] Does the existence of this dispute indicate that international law influences behavior? If the German Democratic Republic and Soviet Union officials had been told by their legal experts (assuming these had been consulted) that there were absolutely no legal grounds for the wall, would there have been no wall?

The popular hunch is that it probably would have made no difference: the political reality of losing two and a half million people from a population of nineteen million, with the almost certain probability that the flow would continue, is undoubtedly the reason for the wall; and legal niceties would not prevent state officials from acting to secure themselves against the disintegration of their state.

This position is persuasive, but one nevertheless wonders to what extent the legal questions were considered in the decision-making process.[16] It would be useful to question the officials to learn if they were part of the predecision thinking. Certainly, these questions arose during postdecision thinking, for a spirited legal defense is part of the present political posture of East German authorities with regard to the wall. The appearance of legal legitimacy was considered important enough to work for. Furthermore, the argument is not that there is no law or that there is improper law; the East Germans and the Soviets are arguing that they have abided by traditional international law.[17]

Turning to another facet of the Berlin problem, what evaluation of the relevance of a legal context can we make of the following? There is the argument that the West should not change the status of Berlin in such a way that its rights of presence and operations would no longer emanate from conquest or belligerent occupation[18] but from a treaty, unless the West is able to achieve a "guaranteed" solution to the total German problem.[19] If Western rights were based on treaty, it is argued, its legal presence would be placed in jeopardy, for it would be easier to construct a colorable legal argument on abrogation of a treaty based on *rebus sic stantibus* than it would be to argue against rights stemming from occupation. Thus, it might be said that legalistic arguments are being used in the formulation of policy in connection with possible negotiations about Berlin. What weight should this be given in determining the role of international law?

One more specific instance of law-affected behavior bears telling. The crisis of 1958 was initiated by Khrushchev in a series of press conferences, speeches, and informal talks, all of which were intended to get the West out of Berlin.[20] What is interesting about his behavior for our purposes is the shift in argument, a shift which seems attributable to his having been in error on a matter of international law. Khrushchev moved from a position of denouncing the West's occupation rights under *rebus sic stantibus,* having assumed they emanated from the Potsdam Agreement,[21] to a position which acknowledged present legality of Western occupation of Berlin under belligerent occupation.[22] His argument then was that the legal presence would terminate once a peace treaty had been signed between the Soviet Union and the German Democratic Republic.[23] Presumably, once such a treaty was consummated, *rebus sic stantibus* would be invoked. The reason for this change of position may not have been solely to correct a legal error but may also have been concerned with the dynamics of the control which Soviet officials exercise over East German foreign policy. Or it may have been thought that a stronger position could be built on alternative arguments, which, in the unlikely circumstance that the Berlin problem would become subject to international adjudication, might be the case. There is, nevertheless, this point to be made: International law does have an impact upon the legal positions taken by states.

The apparent rhetorical redundancy of this proposition should not obscure the point that those who make legal arguments must necessarily use legal rhetoric. We should remind ourselves that the Soviets could refuse to use international law, speak in terms of and use only "socialist" or "peaceful coexistence" international law, or not refer to any kind of law. But, as has been noted, Soviet Union officials do and are likely to continue to make use of international law justifications for their actions. To be sure, their use of the law is highly selective, but there can be no argument that once they have chosen to invoke it within a particular context, it is difficult, if not impossible, to deny its invocation by other states for the same situation. As a result, it may even be difficult for the Soviets to deny the validity of invoking international law in situations in which they choose not to do so.

This illustration, then, is useful to suggest still another way in which international law may be said to have been relevant to the events of West Berlin. It has provided a stabilizing rhetoric. The generalized argument goes something like this: When officialdom from nation-states meet to negotiate with one another, there must be some means of communication: if, for example, they bring to the negotiation table a rhetoric of invective ("war-mongers," "revanchists"), this is likely to exacerbate tensions and accentuate conflict. If, on the other hand, they bring to the negotiations a rhetoric which fragments the overriding tensions into classifiable and specific issues, or a way of talking about disputes within a tradition of attempts to resolve conflict, it adds to the possibility of peaceful settlement. A common legal terminology, when accompanied by agreed-upon procedures for discussion, may provide face-saving opportunities for substantive discussion or merely time to look for alternative solutions. To be sure, we need more study of the tolerance range and set of circumstances within which this stabilizing rhetoric is useful in avoiding conflict. As in some of the instances noted above, this may turn out to be a very limited area. But perhaps a study of this feature of international law will suggest more efficient ways to make use of it.[24]

Thus far, we have looked at four instances in our attempt to evaluate the extent to which international law is relevant to the events surrounding Berlin. Upon reviewing our analyses of these instances, it may be seen that we have been operating with three dimensions of a limited methodological scheme: (1) the kind of activity upon which international law norms may be relevant; (2) the manner in which these norms may have been operative upon this activity; and (3) the type, in terms of sources of international law, of norms which may have been operative. If pursued seriously, the use of these dimensions would produce a series of proposi-

111

tions that would describe how a range of activity (from overt individual behavior to decision-making by a policy elite) had been influenced (for example, determined, guided, or rationalized) by various international law norms (categorized according to authoritative source).[25] But within the limited scheme here undertaken, permit me a conclusion addressed to those holding that international law has had little impact upon the events of Berlin: International law norms have had a far greater impact upon the behavior of governments than that attitude would allow. The day-to-day contacts of the various state officials in Berlin were certainly controlled by these norms in the instances already reviewed, and there is good reason to believe that policy-makers in both the East and West were acutely aware of international law even in those instances where they might have intended to disregard or violate it. A persuasive, if somewhat extravagant, argument could be made that not only has international law been controlling in the periods between the three crises (the airlift of 1948, the crisis of 1958 with its six-month ultimatum, and the wall of 1961), but that the type of actions taken both to modify existing relations and to reduce the crisis to some stability were in part determined by the existing body of international law norms.

Notwithstanding all of this, however, I must confess an inclination to side with the skeptics—especially if, as I suspect to be the case, much of their attitude is directed against the way in which international law is typically studied and presented. I am well aware of the classic illustrations of diplomatic and consular immunities, of the law of the seas and an unbroken line of treaties and arbitration judgments, as well as of the conduct of routine matters between states and the sometimes tortured analyses of UN action to which teachers of international law have pointed to convince their students and themselves that international law is indeed operative. Nor am I likely to give up my commitment to that set of lectures which provides those illustrations. At the same time, I believe that much of what is done by international-law scholars is not relevant—not relevant in the sense that it does not come to grips with the central problem of our era, the prevention of war and the establishment of a peace system for international relations.

In supporting this position I should like to make clear that my emphasis is focused on the relatively distinct or characteristic contribution which law and the person trained in legal skills may make toward solving this problem. With this understood, let me add some specificity to this charge. Stated affirmatively, the cardinal canon of relevancy in connection with question construction, investigation procedures, and standards of persuasion and demonstration for international legal scholarship is the necessity of relating these activities to the primary issue of war prevention. If one were to ask if such a canon implied the neglect of all the traditional subjects of international law which do not easily relate to this issue, or more subtly, if investigation of these traditional subjects does not actually contribute to the development of a peace system, the only reasonable reply would be to acknowledge that the canon is somewhat overstated. Furthermore, it must be acknowledged that there are a number of scholars who are working with war prevention as their central topic. But let us be unreasonable and pursue the matter a little further. Given the magnitude and urgency of the task, it can be fairly argued that there are too few in the legal profession who take war prevention as their primary issue, and those who do, work with a framework that is inappropriate for the task.

To be sure, there are clear indications of a general recognition among international-law scholars of the urgency for direction of the present international system. Most see the need to accommodate legal norms to the increasingly rapid and unpredictable changes in the social and economic organization of international politics and are aware that such accommodation requires a greater operational use of the relationship of international law to the international political system. In addition, most responsible scholars would welcome and probably work for a strengthening of the United Nations. Many would undoubtedly be receptive to a significant curtailment of unilateral action or national sovereignty if it would assure war prevention and the establishment of a peace system. And while it is not yet either intellectually or politically respectable to advocate world government, there may even be several serious scholars who would agree with Pope John XXIII's assertion that the nation-state system of international relations is no longer capable of dealing with the problems of peace and security and that some superseding authority has to be created to prevent international conflicts.[26]

Yet there is a sense in which all of us go about our work which belies these realizations. By and large, scholars structure problems in a way which provides support for an unreliable method of achieving and maintaining a peaceful world. I shall try to support this admittedly difficult contention within the context of the Berlin problem.

After the erection of the wall, the American Journal of International Law published a comment on the crisis by Professor Quincy Wright [27] and a reply to Professor Wright's position by Ambassador Wilhelm G. Grewe.[28] Professor Wright moves surely and easily through traditional international law to establish the points that there is no legal objection to the Soviet Union's recognition of East Germany; that there is no legal objection to a peace treaty between these two states; and that should the latter situation come to pass, the West could not legally be deprived of its enclave in West Berlin. Professor Wright's analysis, although brief, also shows that he is clearly aware of the political realities of the situation. He suggests a return to Potsdam (a political, not a legal solution, which the Russians have long advocated), noting that a disarmed, neutralized Germany would probably have a Western orientation.

Ambassador Grewe answers each of the points made by Professor Wright in as competent and persuasive a fashion. East Germany is not a *de facto* state since it lacks the minimum of effective authority required by international law to make recognition permissible. For the Soviet Union to conclude a peace treaty with the GDR would be in violation of the 1945 agreements which are still in full effect since the Western powers have not concluded peace treaties with West Germany. If recognition were accorded the GDR and a peace treaty concluded, West Berlin would not become an enclave but a separate international entity, leaving the concept of Germany shattered into three remnants. A return to Potsdam is unrealistic, for this was the policy that caused the division of Germany.

While there are certainly grounds for preferring one position to another, it is difficult to avoid the impression that these are opposing briefs for a matter such as a corporate proxy fight and where, as is usual in Anglo-American law, two lines of doctrine are available to the parties.

Of course, the formality of style, the common rhetoric and doctrines, and the notion of relevant argument within defined substantive areas and techniques make up the stabilizing rhetoric which gives contemporary international law some of its bite. That may be a sufficient reason to maintain its present form. Yet my own position would be that this posture of reasoned argumentation falls so far short of what is needed within the present situation that it might be more sensible to dispense with it. To my mind, legal analysis of contemporary international conflicts, especially if they involve super-power confrontation or a potentiality of international violence, is insufficient unless it specifically explores how, if issues were decided in a particular fashion, a more stable and peaceful world would result.

A peaceful world is probably what Professor Wright had in mind, and it is possible to perceive the argument he might make to show where his suggestions would lead: the Soviet Union has reason to fear a united Germany linked with NATO; the West must realize this and make its realization known to the Soviets; recognition of East Germany would be a manifestation of such a realization, but at the same time there are human and symbolic reasons for retaining the enclave in West Berlin. It follows, then, that a combination of recognition and firmness on West Berlin would aid stability and peace in that the appropriate mixture of accommodation and strength would show Allied willingness to relax tensions without relaxing its guard. From this might emerge some political rearrangement which might encompass disengagement and even disarmament.

The logic of Ambassador Grewe's objections to Professor Wright's legal position suggests that his view as to what is needed for a peaceful world involves the following: the German people are insistent upon a unified Germany, and until this is accomplished they constitute an unsettling force discontented with present political facts and will be looking for opportunities to bring about the necessary changes. What steps they (referring to the previously mentioned Germans) might follow and how far they would go is difficult to infer from the note.

No matter what may be one's predilections with regard to these two "peace" analyses, this is the kind of analysis we should demand from international legal scholars. In this way, their use of legal doctrine would become directly relevant to the crucial issue of war prevention in an operational fashion.

There are some ready objections to this program. To begin with, it asks that everyone become a political analyst. It is obvious that not everyone is equipped to do this; there is the concomitant difficulty that understanding international behavior is frequently difficult and sometimes impossible. Under these circumstances, is it not more sensible to plod ahead with traditional legal analyses, attempting thereby to give some structure to otherwise overwhelming events? But whether articulated or not, any legal analysis assumes some image of political processes and international relations. Political analysis, then, cannot be avoided: it can only be done advertently or inadvertently, poorly or well. But the point should be pressed even further. If, as I believe, responsible individuals must now undertake the enormous task of moving from a war-prone to a war-prevention system of international relations, it will become a serious enterprise only to the extent that there is a conscious attempt to interject peace analyses. The attempt to eliminate international violence demands a radical change in social life, and our inability to escape from habits of thought and modes of investigation which are interwoven into a war-prone system is very profound. Carrying on as usual—relying on traditional methods of stating the problems, investigating, and offering solutions with appropriate authority—seems to me to be hopelessly inadequate for the task.

I shall return to the objections to a consciously directed peace analysis as an operational context for legal scholarship, but let me first attempt to give some additional substance, slight as it may be, to what this program would entail. The late Secretary-General, Dag Hammarskjöld, analyzed the role of the United Nations in matters where the superpowers are in direct confrontation with specific mention of Berlin. In his last annual report to the organization, he wrote the following:

> What is true of the disarmament problem is, of course, true also of those more specific questions in which security interests of big powers are or may be directly involved, as for example the Berlin problem. The community of nations, represented in the United Nations, has a vital interest in a peaceful solution, based on justice, of any question which—like this one—unless brought to a satisfactory solution, might come to represent a threat to peace and security. However, the problem of the balance to be struck between the rights and obligations of the big powers and the rights and obligations of all other nations applies, in a very direct way, also to this problem which is now so seriously preoccupying the minds of all peoples and their leaders. The United Nations, with its wide membership, is not, and can, perhaps, not aspire to be a focal point in the debate on an issue such as the Berlin question, or in the efforts to solve it, but the Organization cannot, for that reason, be considered as an outside party which has no right to make its voice heard should a situation develop which would threaten those very interests which the United Nations is to safeguard

and for the defense of which it was intended to provide all member nations with an instrument and a forum.[29]

Hammarskjöld saw the direct interest of the organization as coming into play only when peace and security were threatened. In other speeches, notably in Copenhagen in 1959,[30] he made it clear that the UN could not be expected to produce the garrison that would actually protect a free city of Berlin, nor could it take over the authority of administering the city. He did, however, indicate that there were other roles it could assume. And in the past few years, the Soviet Union has shown increased interest in UN participation in Berlin, but always in a form that made Western leaders see a threat to either their occupation rights or the maintenance of a truly free city.[31] The Allies have responded with suggestions for international controls for access routes and submission of occupancy rights to international adjudication.[32] (In the light of the United States position on the jurisdiction of the international court, the latter suggestion must have seemed quite hypocritical.) At any rate, an international access authority was never given a fair chance due to other issues which arose and might arise again.

None of this really comes to grips with the question of what use could be made of international organization when superpowers confront one another. A paper of limited circulation by Louis Henkin [33] explores the problem in some depth within the Berlin context, but it seems to be the only available detailed analysis. In brief, he regards contribution to the success of negotiations between East and West as the most realistic and effective task the United Nations could undertake. Although it is unlikely that war would erupt over Berlin, the UN could do little to prevent or mitigate it. Its role in any case is secondary, so long as negotiations hold some promise. Within this scope, while recognizing that the Big Powers are the efficient operators, he outlines a series of actions and roles for which the United Nations could prepare itself.[34] I do not know that it has done so.

But is this, or should it be, the end of legal analyses of the UN function? Why should not international lawyers be openly programmatic and investigate, for example, the way in which the General Assembly or other appropriate organs should plan for specific actions with reference to Berlin: how and under what circumstances should a token force be selected and trained and for what functions? What would be the consequences of moving a UN organ to Berlin and how could this be done? The answer to why serious programmatic study is not undertaken might be a mistaken notion that this is not "law." But in actuality, such activity is a very real part of a lawyer's function. "Commercial" lawyers are constantly called upon to make judgments about business deals, advertising campaigns, applicants for positions. They have a role in such affairs, not merely because they are considered men of good judgment, but because the lawyer's knowledge of the legal framework of the company he is advising gives him a special insight into such "extralegal" problems.

International lawyers, whose client is peace, will serve that client well only if they provide direction on matters heretofore considered "purely political." [35] I believe that it has become increasingly clear that without centralized peace-keeping and conflict-resolution machinery, it is unlikely that we will reach the year 2000 without a major holocaust. If this is so, we need a good deal more attention to how this machinery should appear and can be obtained. This means we need to pay more attention to the relation of a developing international law to a vertical, rather than to a horizontal, international structure.[36] The lawyer who has peace as a client, with specific reference to Berlin, must find some way, when agreement comes near, to convince the parties to add an extra measure of vertical organization. To do this will require some thought now; otherwise we shall settle for whatever relieves the momentary tension and will not or shall not be able to build our stabilizing structures.

Two more objections remain to be considered. First, peace is not our only objective. The second, put simply, is, "Just what are you talking about?"

I do not deny that I find the first troublesome, for I have struggled with the conflict of values involved. Many in our society who have been faced with a choice have resolved the conflict in favor of the preservation of our way of life as our only object. Their threshold for war is, therefore, lower, so that the "hawks" (to mislabel them) may see no alternative but pre-emptive war in any given situation. But I think it is possible for the responsible elite in the major societies to plan for periods of crisis so that the hawks are not given their wings. Each major group is aware that the others are, like itself, split into subgroups of "hawks" and "doves." The decision-makers should plan a policy designed to have an impact supporting the "doves" in the other societies. To do so, they should be aware of the full range of activities through which such influence could be brought to bear. Tacit support of the pro-peace elite could be planned through unilateral, bilateral, and international structures. Such planning should begin with the value conflict itself, which I shall phrase in McDougal's terminology as the law of human dignity against the law of human indignity.[37] While I disagree with the line he draws between dignity and indignity, I must acknowledge that describing a line is difficult. Certainly the choice between the law which permits us to stay in West Berlin and protect its two million inhabitants and the law which demands that we get out and run the risk that they will fall under the heel of what appears to be a terribly depressed, if not oppressed, society (East Germany) poses the problem squarely. My only answer is that I hope we have the ingenuity and persistence to effectuate a stable minimum world order and retain as much dignity as possible.

That I have offered no concrete solution certainly leads to the next objection: "Just what are you talking about?" Is it not true that all this talk about a war-prevention system has not provided us with one answer which our present methods would not have yielded eventually? Isn't it true that war-prevention is a globular concept which glosses over what needs to be seen: that we live in a time in which the nation-state law is our only law, especially where the major powers are concerned? If we add to this law of nations the presence of the United Nations and some notion of the stabilities and instabilities of a nuclear deterrent system, we are as likely to come to valid conclusions about war prevention as we are when starting with a perspective labelled war-prevention. Where is the novelty, if not the utility, of what has been suggested?

But how successful have the perspectives not labelled war-prevention been in solving the Berlin problem. Certainly it is fair to argue on purely empirical grounds that these perspectives have not revealed in even an approximate way the impact the present international legal structure is having on the events surrounding Berlin and that some decent research on the behavioral level is sorely needed. In addition, I do not see that the attempt to use either a traditional positivistic analysis, or a Kelsenian, or a sophisticated political-legal perspective leads to any particular set of conclusions, although I would not deny that research into past episodes or hard analysis from one of these perspectives might illuminate some facet of the problem. But these traditional perspectives are methodological approaches, not tied to war prevention or any relevant ideology. Not being peace-oriented, these methods have not led us to a substantive consideration of the mutual balance of terror. What I am talking about is that legal scholars, in looking for a war-prevention system by which to move toward a warless world, need to develop a new set of priorities for legal thought. Most simply put, an analysis of the legality of occupation rights in Berlin is less important than the development of peace-keeping machinery and conflict-resolution devices, especially when dealing with the superpowers. I do not say that traditional approaches have not touched on these matters or that in the past nineteen years almost everything a war-prevention theorist may think of has not been said by someone. I do say, however, that with this set of priorities and a talent better than mine, we may yet create a model sufficiently untangled from the past that a future is possible.[38]

We are all aware that even in domestic law, much of life is what we say it is or make it. What is part and parcel of our stock-in-trade in international law is the knowledge that what we say is law has a real chance of becoming law. What I have been saying here is that a war-preventive legal structure is the only relevant structure for the problem of West Berlin. Hopefully, this "saying so" will help to make it so.

1. The conference was held in March, 1963, in Brookline, Massachusetts under the auspices of the American Friends Committee.

2. The panel consisted of three competent and distinguished scholars: Louis Coser, Professor of Sociology at Brandeis University, whose interest is the sociology of conflict and who had just recently returned from a trip to Poland and Yugoslavia; Stuart Hughes, Professor of Modern European History at Harvard University; and Fritz Ringer, Assistant Professor of German at Harvard University.

3. For a general discussion of the range of positions on Berlin and the problems of Germany, see an excellent review of six books, Shell, *Book Review,* 16 WORLD POLITICS 137 (October, 1963).

4. There was brief comment on the Potsdam and Yalta conferences, a passing reference to some difficulty with the Four Power Military Control Agreement, and a casual suggestion that a United Nations "presence" might be used in connection with the guaranteed status of Berlin, but none of these were developed at length.

5. Perhaps it should be noted that the moderator of the panel identified the questioner as a professor of international law. I bother to detail this because it seemed the panelists attempted to provide serious and responsible answers befitting questions emanating from such a status.

6. STAFF OF SENATE COMM. ON FOREIGN RELATIONS, 88th CONG., 1ST SESS., REPORT ON BERLIN IN A CHANGING EUROPE 1–2 (Comm. Print 1963). Senators Mike Mansfield, J. Caleb Boggs, Claiborne Pell, and Benjamin A. Smith visited Germany in December, 1962, and this is a report of their findings.

7. For a survey of events before and after the erection of the wall, which was begun on August 13, 1961, see Barker, *The Berlin Crisis 1958–62,* 39 INT'L AFF. 59 (1963).

8. The recognition of a state has been defined as " . . . the free act by which one or more States acknowledge the existence on a definite territory of a human society politically organised, independent of any other existing State, and capable of observing the obligations of international law, and by which they manifest therefore their intention to consider it a member of the international community." Institute of International Law, *Resolutions adopted at Brussels in 1936,* 30 AM. J. INT'L L. 185 (Supp. 1936).

"Recognition as a Government, on the other hand, implies that the recognised Government is, in the opinion of the recognising State, qualified to represent an existing State." STARKE, AN INTRODUCTION TO INTERNATIONAL LAW 123 (5th ed. 1963).

9. See 1 HACKWORTH, DIGEST OF INTERNATIONAL LAW chap. iii (1940); LAUTERPACHT, RECOGNITION IN INTER-

NATIONAL LAW (1947); 2 WHITEMAN, DIGEST OF INTERNATIONAL LAW chap. iii (1963).

10. Recognition may be formal or implied. *De jure* recognition may ordinarily be implied only when there is an unequivocal manifestation of intent to establish formal relations with the new state or government. A state, however, may lay itself open to the inference that it has recognized another state or government by entering into some kind of relations with it. "Such conduct can usually amount to no more than recognition *de facto,* or recognition of an entity as an insurgent authority, or indicate an intention to maintain, through agents, informal relations without recognition." STARKE, *op. cit. supra* note 8, at 127 (1963). The legal effects of recognition are discussed *id.* at 139.

When the Test Ban Treaty was signed, there were some expressions of concern that East Germany's subscription to a treaty signed by the United States would amount to tacit recognition by the latter of the German Democratic Republic. The Department of State issued a statement that such a result would not follow: " . . . it is a well-established proposition of international law that recognition is not accorded to an unrecognized regime when that regime acts to become a party to a multilateral treaty along with states that do not recognize it. Similarly, such action by an unrecognized regime does not result in any recognition or acknowledgment of the existence of the state which the regime purports to govern.

"Diplomatic recognition of a government and also recognition or acknowledgment of the existence of a state is a matter of intention. No government is held to recognize unless it intends to do so.

"The United States does not recognize that East Germany constitutes a state." 49 DEP'T STATE BULL. 355 (1963).

11. 1 SCHWARZENBERGER, A MANUAL OF INTERNATIONAL LAW 61–62 (4th ed. 1960).

12. The United States bases its objection to restrictions on movement in East Berlin on postwar agreements. Part of the text of a U.S. note of protest to the Soviet Ministry of Foreign Affairs on July 5, 1963, read as follows: "The East German authorities have no competence for Berlin and these measures are completely illegal. They aggravate the arbitrary actions taken since August 13, 1961, by these authorities in

connection with the Soviet Government which have cut the city in two by construction of the 'wall.' These latest illegal measures constitute a serious infringement of the quadripartite status of Berlin as established in the agreements of 1944 and 1945. They not only purport to limit the right of the Allies to circulate freely in Greater Berlin, but also, together with similar measures taken outside Berlin, constitute in their effects another brutal violation of the most elementary rights of the German population." 49 DEP'T STATE BULL. 138 (1963).

These agreements were also the basis of United States protest against the erection of the wall and the limitations on movement imposed concurrently: "All this is a flagrant, and particularly serious, violation of the quadripartite status of Berlin. Freedom of movement with respect to Berlin was reaffirmed by the quadripartite agreement of New York of May 4, 1949, and by the decision taken at Paris on June 20, 1949. . . . The United States Government has never accepted that limitations can be imposed on freedom of movement within Berlin." Note from the American Embassy at Moscow to the Soviet Foreign Ministry Concerning Violation of the Quadripartite Status of Berlin, [1961] STAFF OF SENATE COMM. ON FOREIGN RELATIONS, op. cit. supra note 6, at 796.

13. Wright, *Some Legal Aspects of the Berlin Crisis,* 55 AM. J. INT'L L. 959, 964 (1961).

14. See Declaration of Warsaw Pact Powers, 45 DEP'T STATE BULL. 400–01 (1961).

15. See Communiqué of Ministerial Meeting of the North Atlantic Council at Paris, [1961] 46 DEP'T OF STATE BULL. 51 (1962).

16. See Decree of the Council of Ministers of the GDR of August 12, 1961 (one day before the erection of the wall): "In order to prevent the unfriendly activities of the revenge-seeking and militaristic powers in Western Germany and West Berlin, a system of control shall be set up at the borders of the GDR, including the border with the Western Sectors of Greater Berlin such as exists on the borders of every sovereign State." Quoted in INTERNATIONAL COMMISSION OF JURISTS, THE BERLIN WALL: A DEFIANCE OF HUMAN RIGHTS 29 (1962).

17. Election speech in East Berlin by Walter Ulbricht concerning West Berlin, [1961] STAFF OF SENATE COMM. ON FOREIGN RELATIONS, *op. cit. supra* note 6, at 796: "For what are we preparing ourselves now? The most important thing in the next few months is the conclusion of a German peace treaty. Connected with it is the establishment of the complete sovereignty of the GDR, a sovereignty which must be respected by all states, and, of this I am convinced, which will eventually in fact be respected.

"Part of this sovereignty is full control over all our routes of communications in exactly the same way as this applies in the case of every sovereign state. Our opponents say in this connection that our absolute claim to control over all routes of communications means impeding the routes of communication. This is obviously malicious nonsense. Control does not mean disturbance, but order; that means order on our routes of communication which corresponds with the generally recognized rules of international law. We want nothing more and nothing less."

18. These are two distinctive theories, it should be noted, held by various states for different political reasons. "Conquest is the acquisition of the territory of an enemy by its complete and final subjugation and a declaration of the conquering state's intention to annex it. In practice a title by conquest is rare, because the annexation of territory after a war is generally carried out by a treaty of cession, although such a treaty often only confirms a title already acquired by conquest." BRIERLY, LAW OF NATIONS 124 (2d ed. 1936). Belligerent or military occupation, on the other hand, has been described as follows: "Being an incident of war, military occupation confers upon the invading force the means of exercising control for the period of occupation. It does not transfer the sovereignty to the occupant, but simply the authority or power to exercise some of the rights of sovereignty. The exercise of these rights results from the established power of the occupant and from the necessity of maintaining law and order, indispensable both to the inhabitants and to the occupying force. It is therefore unlawful for a belligerent occupant to annex occupied territory or to create a new State therein while hostilities are still in progress." U.S. DEP'T OF THE ARMY, THE LAW OF LAND WARFARE, FM 27–10 (1956).

19. See Morgenthau, *The Problem of German Reunification,* 330 Annals 124, 128 (1960). Compare NEAL, WAR AND PEACE AND GERMANY 110–16 (1962).

20. Barker, *The Berlin Crisis 1958-62,* 32 INT'L AFF. 59, 60–61 (1963).

21. Address by Premier Khrushchev at a Soviet-Polish Meeting, on Germany and Berlin, [1958] STAFF OF SENATE COMM. ON FOREIGN RELATIONS, *op. cit. supra* note 6, at 339–43; Note from the Soviet Foreign Ministry to the American Ambassador at Moscow (Thompson) Regarding Berlin, [1958] *id.* at 348, 354–55.

22. Address by Premier Khrushchev to a Rally in East Berlin, [1959] *id.* at 431–36. Khrushchev here did not tie occupation rights to Potsdam but denounced them as "abnormal" fourteen years after the war's end. He also urged the signing of a peace treaty. *Id.* at 432.

23. See Morgenthau, *The Problem of German Reunification,* 330 ANNALS 124, 127–28 (1960).

24. It should be noted that this point has been made the basis of an ambitious role for law. Arthur Larson has ferreted out the legal issues in the Berlin situation with the notion that by doing so, international adjudication could become the method for providing a firm legal foundation for the solution of political problems. LARSON, WHEN NATIONS DISAGREE 102–06 (1961). While what has been said here seems to buttress Larson's approach, the analysis in the remaining half of this essay should make clear the significant differences between his approach and the one espoused here.

25. I attempted in some rough form to do this for the period from 1945 through March, 1963, but found that, even when approached in a simplistic fashion, it was too much of a task for one person. Without some systematic and reliable count or measurement, it is difficult to state conclusions demanding credence from the reader.

26. POPE JOHN XXIII, PACEM IN TERRIS, Part IV. " . . . the public authorities of the individual nations . . . are no longer capable of facing the task of finding an adequate solution to the [international] problems mentioned above.

"It can be said, therefore, that at this historical moment the present system of organization and the way its principle of authority operate on a world basis no longer correspond

to the objective requirements of the universal common good."
Id., para. 134–35. "Today the universal common good poses
problems of worldwide dimensions which cannot be adequately
tackled or solved except by the efforts of public authorities
endowed with a wideness of powers, structure, and means
of the same proportions, that is, of public authorities which
are in a position to operate in an effective manner on a
worldwide basis. The moral order itself, therefore, demands
that such a form of public authority be established." *Id.,* para.
137. See also RIGA, PEACE ON EARTH, A COMMENTARY ON
POPE JOHN'S ENCYCLICAL 20–21 (1964).

27. Wright, *Some Legal Aspects of the Berlin Crisis,* 55
AM. J. INT'L L. 959 (1961).

28. Grewe, *Other Legal Aspects of the Berlin Crisis,* 56
AM. J. INT'L L. 510 (1962).

29. U.N. GEN. ASS. OFF. REC. 16th Sess., Supp. No. 1A
(1961).

30. Address by Dag Hammarskjöld before the Student's
Association, Copenhagen, Denmark, [1959] 5 U.N. REV. 22
(1959).

31. Soviet Aide Memoire of June 4, [1961] 45 DEP'T
STATE BULL. 231 (1961); Barker, *supra* note 21, at 68, 71.

32. State Department Statement on International Authority to Control Berlin Access Routes, 46 DEP'T STATE BULL.
463 (1962); Barker, *supra* note 21, at 70. In President
Kennedy's Report to the Nation on the Berlin Crisis, July 25,
1961, he stated that the United States was ready to submit
the legality of its rights in Berlin to "international adjudication." 45 DEP'T STATE BULL. 267, 272 (1961). HENKIN,
THE BERLIN CRISIS AND THE UNITED NATIONS 27 (1959)
evaluated resort by the parties to the ICJ and concluded
such a move would be beneficial to the West's position. But
compare his statement, *id.* at 13, as to the obstacles to such
a move with Statement by Secretary Rusk during an Address
at Washington, D. C., on July 10, 1961, 45 DEP'T STATE
BULL. 175, 180 (1961).

33. HENKIN, THE BERLIN CRISIS AND THE UNITED NA-
TIONS (1959).

34. *Id.* at 16–28. Henkin outlines roles the UN might
play in the eventuality the parties to the crisis agree that the

organization should have a part in the settlement of Berlin; in the eventuality that negotiations continue but no agreement is reached; and in the eventuality that the negotiations fail.

35. Serious attention by lawyers to the problems heretofore considered purely political might incidentally have the salutary impact of providing those who will have to offer written drafts of treaties, codes, resolutions, or recommendations with the kind of information which makes for shrewder, more acceptable, and, therefore, more workable instruments.

36. Richard A. Falk, *International Jurisdiction: Horizontal and Vertical Conception of Legal Order,* 32 TEMP. L. Q. 295 (1959).

37. McDougal, *Perspectives for an International Law of Human Dignity,* 58 AM. SOC. INT'L L. PROC. 107 (1959).

38. A model for the Berlin problem has been constructed by James P. Warburg which is a good example of the sort of thing policy-makers and international-law scholars should have in mind when studying that or other crisis situations. Mr. Warburg argues that "standing firm" can only result in a continued risk of war or bit-by-bit attrition of our position in Berlin. Therefore, the United States and Great Britain should take the initiative with a positive solution which must also encompass the larger problem of Germany's future. Negotiations on such a proposal would be based on Russia's removing the oppressive Ulbricht regime and the establishment of a moderate communist government. The West would then offer the following four–point proposal:

a. The West would admit of the *de facto* existence of the GDR and the Oder-Neisse line. The independent German states would be admitted to the UN. They would have ten years to find their own way, without interference, to unification.

b. During this period, all of Berlin is to be considered the potential capital of a united Germany and placed under UN protection, the present garrisons being retained as UN agents. Access is to be guaranteed. NATO and Warsaw powers are not to use their sectors as subversive bases. A UN Berlin Commission will settle disputes.

c. If a decision to unite is made within the ten years, the two states will withdraw from their respective military alliances and the united Germany will be permanently barred from joining any military alliance whatsoever. All foreign troops will leave, including the UN agents, and Berlin will become the capital.

d. If reunification does not take place within the ten years and Berlin is left in the center of a permanently separate GDR, the following will take place with respect to West Berlin: (a) West Berliners who so desire will be given ample time and freedom to remove themselves and their movable belongings to the Federal Republic. (b) The GDR will compensate them for privately owned immovables at values established by the UN Berlin Commission. (c) Publicly owned property in the Western Sectors will be acquired by the GDR from the Federal Republic either by purchase or exchange of territory contiguous to the Federal Republic, the values to be determined as in (b). WARBURG, WHAT TO DO ABOUT BERLIN (1962).

It should be noted that this model is a transitional model; that is, the emphasis is not upon the maintenance of a warless world, but upon how to get from our present war-prone system to a less war-prone system. However, a careful analysis of Mr. Warburg's over-all plan indicates clearly that this transitional model has been directed by his over-all conception of a warless world. In this connection, see his book, DISARMAMENT: THE CHALLENGE OF THE NINETEEN SIXTIES (1961).